Cameos from
of Thomas

A Long
Engagement
1878—1881

Pamela Lomax

Shears & Hogg Publications

Series Title: Cameos from the Life & Times of Thomas Cooper Gotch
Title: A Long Engagement
Author and Editor: Pamela Lomax
Published by Shears & Hogg Publications
Printed by Headland Printers Ltd., Penzance, Cornwall.

First Published 2002
© Shears & Hogg Publications
ISBN 0-9540249-1-5

Shears & Hogg Publications
Wheal Betsy
Chywoone Hill
Newlyn
Cornwall TR18 5AP
Cameo@tcgotch.co.uk

Contents

Prologue   1

    The Slade School of Art   2

    The Shakespeare Reading Club   3

    Caroline Burland Yates   3

A Long Engagement by Thomas Cooper Gotch   6

Deconstructing the Story   13

    Heatherley's Art School   13

    Dating the Story   14

    Jane Ross   17

    The Etching Studio   19

Diversions   20

    Torquay and Falmouth   22

    Abraham and Isaac   23

    Etching at the Slade   24

Art and Life: the Debate   30

    The Pioneers   30

    The Naïve Willie   32

    Monseigneur Love   37

    Santley and his Daughters   40

    Friendships with Men   45

    Samuel Butler   46

    Last Days at the Slade   48

    Butler and Tuke   49

The Maria Tuke Saga   51

    Holiday at Beaumaris   53

    Tennyson's Prince   55

    The Move to Paris   59

    The Saga Continues   60

    Christmas 1880   62

    Facing-up   63

Epilogue   68

    Acknowledgements & Thanks   72

    Bibliography   73

    List of Works by Thomas Cooper Gotch 1877-1881   73

    Index of Names   75

ILLUSTRATIONS

Front cover   Portrait of Caroline Gotch, oil on canvas, 1882. Private collection.

Figure 1. Thomas Cooper Gotch, self portrait.   4
Figure 2. Frontispiece of original manuscript.   5
Figure 3. Jane Ross, self portrait   18
Figure 4. Harry Tuke, self portrait.   22
Figure 5. Abraham & Isaac with Angel by T. C. Gotch   25
Figure 6. Etching of Head of Youth by T. C. Gotch   27
Figure 7. Etching of Head of Man by T. C. Gotch   27
Figure 8. Etching of La Belle Dame Sans Merci
        by T. C. Gotch   28
Figure 9. Etching of Pine Trees with Artist Painting
        by T. C. Gotch   29
Figure 10. William Samuel Tuke by H. S. Tuke   33
Figure 11. Monseigneur Love by T. C. Gotch   38
Figure 12. 'We all sat over the fire for half an hour, Bo
        holding my coat while I dried my breeches'.
        (Sketch from Tuke letter)   41
Figure 13. Photograph of Charles Gogin   47
Figure 14. Photograph of Maria Tuke   53
Figure 15. Sketch of Jessie Gotch by T. C. Gotch   54
Figure 16. Marriage Certificate of T. C. Gotch
        and C. B. Yates   71

Back cover   Detail from Portrait of Caroline Gotch

Prologue

The portrait on the front cover is that of Caroline Gotch. The life-size oil painting shows Carrie in a dark blue/navy dress with gold and white cuffs and collar. She has a decorative rope around the waist and wears a hat. Her left side and full face are towards the viewer. Beneath a dado rail is a frieze decorated with mythological figures. The painting is dated 1882 and was painted by Carrie's husband, Thomas Cooper Gotch when they were in France, living at Brolles near Paris. The painting shows Carrie when she was pregnant with her one and only child Phyllis.

The painting was a valued family possession; an old photograph of the interior of Penwith, the house that Tom and Carrie built in Shottermill, shows it proudly displayed on the drawing room wall. From there it moved with them to Wheal Betsy, the house they built in Newlyn, Cornwall where they remained until first Tom and then Carrie died. From Caroline, the painting passed to her daughter Phyllis and from Phyllis to her daughter Pat. The present owners found it standing against a barn wall covered in bird droppings with the head of a small dog looking through a large hole in Caroline's dress.

Nothing has been written about the romance that brought Tom and Carrie together for a life-long relationship that seems to have strengthened with the passage of time. They met and married while they were students, but the date and place of their first meeting are not recorded. It is possible that their paths crossed at Heatherley's Art School but Caroline joined the School early in 1878 when Tom was spending six months at the Ecole des Beaux Arts in Antwerp. At the end of his stay in Antwerp, he returned to England and spent some further weeks at Heatherley's before finally leaving. During the months before he started at the Slade, he was a student of Samuel Lawrence the portrait painter but his friends from Heatherley's continued to be the main focus of his social life. It is inconceivable that he was not introduced to Caroline during this time; but Tom had experienced a bruising time at the Ecole des Beaux Arts, where his confidence had been shattered and his time in London during the summer of 1878 was full of self-doubt, social experimentation and family rows.

The Slade School of Art

Tom started at the Slade in the autumn of 1878. He was 23 years of age. Carrie, who was the same age as Tom, did not become a student there until January 1879. The Slade School of Art had opened in 1871 as part of University College and was situated in Gower Street. Alphonse Legros had become the professor in 1878. He was French in origin, 'a thick set figure of medium height, with a massive head, slightly bald, black curling hair and beard, and of a rather sombre and lowering expression.' [1]

He was a portrait painter, a social realist. His figurative paintings often had a strong religious element; women at prayer were a constant theme and for these he drew upon religious ceremonies and monastic life. He believed in helping young artists to develop their individuality by making them use their heads rather than slavishly copying.

Tom would have started in 'the antique', with Mr Durham. He would have worked in a crowded room, amid a jumble of easels and students of all abilities, with girls more numerous than the fellows. Tom would have warmed immediately to the delicate line work with the pale grey Italian chalk that Legros preferred to the stumped and fully shaded drawing that Charles Verlat, the professor in Antwerp had thought was a better training and preparation for tone and colour. Legros objected to reflected light in workmanship, because it prevented students from seeing broadly, and he disliked drawings that became dark. From Antwerp, Tom had written in disgust,

> 'instead of lynx-eyed stippling behold great smudges with a leather stump, or coarse scribblings with the point; feet with the very faintest indications of the toes, and really the gayest disregard for any detail I think I cannot see!' [2]

There is little indication in the correspondence from this period that Tom socialised with other students at the Slade during the autumn of 1878. This is surprising as other evidence suggests that he was an attractive, outgoing young man, well liked by the people he met. Perhaps self-doubt about his calling as an artist, which was a recurring theme in his letters, still existed. In the six months in London as a student of Lawrence, Tom had explored the possibility of making a ca-

1.   Jacomb-Hood, 1925:11

2.   Letter from T. C. Gotch to Jane Ross, 18th November 1877

reer as a preacher or a writer. These doubts might have impeded the formation of new friendships with other artists. The weather did not help; Walter Sparrow, a student at this time, described how they worked by gaslight for nearly the whole of that autumn term of 1878. The fogs, made worse by the smoke from the belching steam engines of the metropolitan railway, were like a mixture of pea soup and soot. [3]

The Shakespeare Reading Club

Tom was already involved with a close-knit group of friends from Heatherley's. Before term started they had formed a Shakespeare reading club. Tom kept a record of club accounts in a small notebook, which is in the Tate Archive. It shows that on the 8th October, nine copies of 'Twelfth Night' were purchased for 9d, on the 15th October, eleven copies of 'Much Ado' for 11d, and on the 24th October, twelve copies of 'Henry IV' for 1/-. The group met in the ballroom at Heatherley's and paid 2/- for the room. By the end of October, thirteen members had paid their subscription of 2/6d. They included Jane Ross, Henrietta Farr, Alma Broadbridge, Harold Rathbone and Henry Paget, who were all at Heatherley's. There was also Tom's brother John Alfred who was studying architecture in London, Jane's brother, and Paget's sister and his two brothers Walter and Sidney. By Christmas, the group had expanded further and included A. Chevallier Tayler who was later to join Tom in Newlyn.

The first concrete evidence that Tom and Carrie had met comes from the entry in Tom's account book at the end of January 1879. The name Caroline Burland Yates is the first name in the list of subscribers for the new term! [4]

Caroline Burland Yates

Caroline lived at 53 Warwick Rd, Maida Vale with her sister, Ess. She was the youngest daughter of Edward Yates, a wealthy gentleman who owned property in various parts of England. She had two sisters, Margaret and Esther (known as Ess). Caroline grew up at the family home, Lammermoor, which was in Sway, on the

3. Sparrow, 1925:89

4. Small notebook kept by T.C.Gotch and containing accounts of the Shakespeare Club from 8th October 1878 until 20th May 1879 (Tate Archive)

edge of the New Forest. She was educated by governesses and later was at school in Switzerland where she learned to speak French fluently and after that at a finishing school in Germany.

Edward Yates was said to have treated Caroline like the son he wanted but did not have. 'He taught her about estate management; about politics; how to fish and how to shoot at a target; how to play whist and poker; and how to select the right wines for different menus.' [5] It is not surprising that when Caroline decided on a career in art that Edward Yates rented a house for her in London.

Little has been written about the courtship of Thomas Cooper Gotch and Caroline Burland Yates. What follows is a detective story. The first clues come from Tom Gotch's undated short story, *A Long Engagement.* [6]

FIGURE 1. THOMAS COOPER GOTCH: SELF PORTRAIT, CIRCA 1879
SOURCE: GOTCH, 2000

5. Handwritten notes on the life of Mrs. Caroline Burland Yates as requested by Lawrence M. Gotch from Maureen de Verdieres Bodilly, her daughter, 1960. (Christopher Gotch Archive).

6. The manuscript is from the Shears Archive.

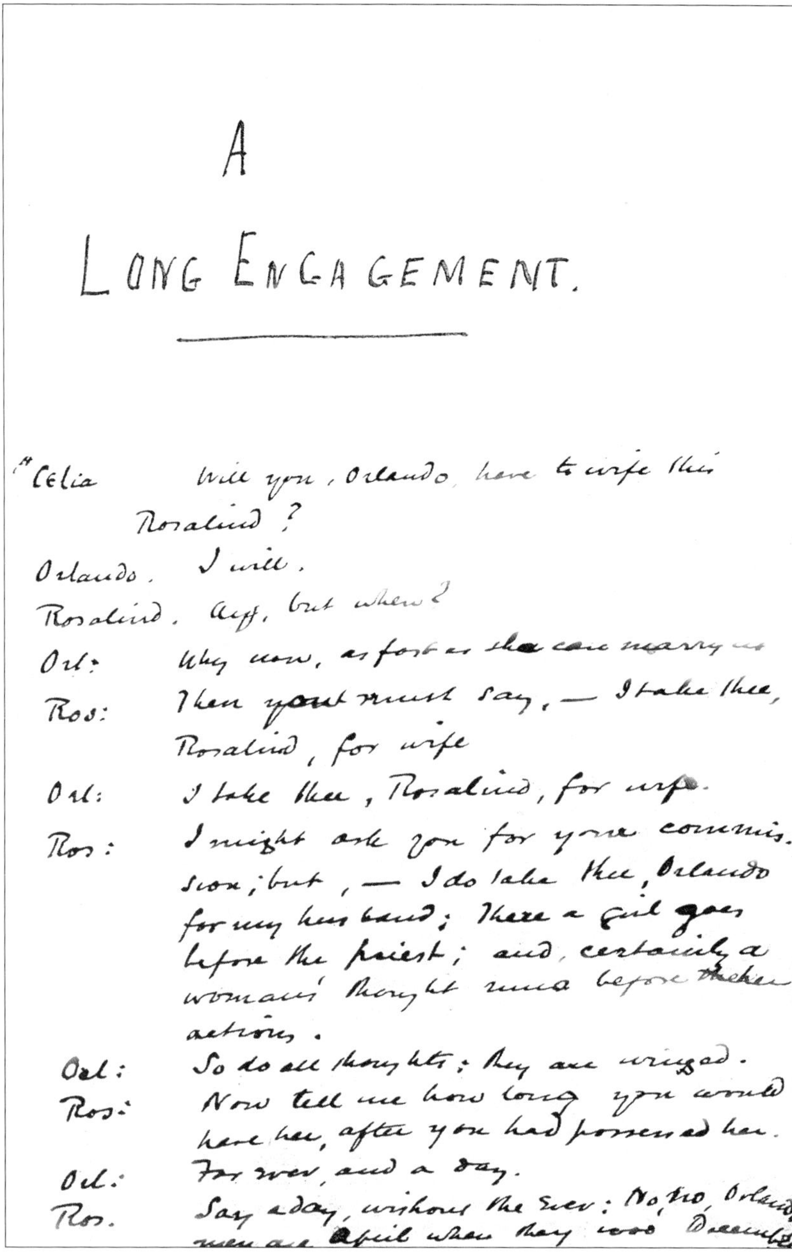

A

LONG ENGAGEMENT.

Celia: Will you, Orlando, have to wife this
Rosalind?

Orlando. I will.

Rosalind. Ay, but when?

Orl: Why now, as fast as she can marry us

Ros: Then you must say, — I take thee,
Rosalind, for wife

Orl: I take thee, Rosalind, for wife.

Ros: I might ask you for your commis-
sion; but, — I do take thee, Orlando
for my husband; there a girl goes
before the priest; and, certainly a
woman's thought runs before their
actions.

Orl: So do all thoughts; they are winged.

Ros: Now tell me how long you would
have her, after you had possessed her.

Orl: For ever, and a day.

Ros. Say a day, without the ever: No, no, Orlando,
men are April when they woo, December

FIGURE 2. FRONTISPIECE OF ORIGINAL MANUSCRIPT
SOURCE: ALAN SHEARS ARCHIVE

A Long Engagement
by Thomas Cooper Gotch

Mistress Marian Thornely was a very advanced young lady; there could be little doubt of that as one watched her painting. At this particular moment she was seated on a high stool some two yards from the model; her dress was of the plainest and hung in simple folds to the ground; a large apron with a rich flowered pattern of dull reds and yellows and the prettiest little frill round her neck, completed her costume; so far she was not unlike many another. But above this was such a head, as an intelligent person would try to catch sight of more than once. Her black hair, quite unconfined, hung like a shaggy mane round her shoulders; her eyes were gentle and sincere in expression and gazed at you beneath straight and well marked eyebrows; her nose and mouth, both firm and well formed, and her dimpled chin, were all justly proportioned; and when she turned to look at one, one felt oneself within the observation of a definite and original person.

The clock in a distant room had struck the half hour a few minutes before and even the most irresponsible students were silently working when there entered the life room – lifting that part of the curtain, which hung across the doorway, and dropping it behind him – a young fellow about two or three and twenty. He turned to one or two lady students and nodded to the men of his acquaintance as one after another turned to see who had entered and began forthwith in a low decided voice to lecture one of his lady friends on her painting, making most emphatic gestures with his thumb. No sooner had he left her with a smile than he was merrily talking to another, chatting with an odd mixture of satire and openness. Again he was disengaged and made his way through the narrow space between the benches, towards Miss Thornely - knocking down a pot of turpentine and a projecting sheaf of brushes on his way. Immediately he turned quite unembarrassed, picked up the brushes with many apologies, saying with a quaint unaffected seriousness, that he hoped that there was some turpentine left. At last he was seated on a low box close by Miss Thornely's easel, well out of someone's way.

'I am afraid you have not been working very hard today Mr Haycroft', said Marian.

'I escaped early' he replied. 'We have been etching all day at the school - see my hands - and there's nothing so tiring as doing masking; really it is quite ridiculous, we stand about or gossip while the varnish dries or while proofs are being printed, making little half-finished idiotic remarks - precisely like youths trying to kill a wet day'.

'It can't be so bad as getting one's picture from the Academy', said Miss Thornely, 'I don't know anything so - so uncomfortable as that'.

'Rejected ones?'

'Yes: I went there for mine yesterday.'

'Did you really? Why didn't you let me know; I would have got yours with pleasure, I have to go for mine'.

'I thought I should like to see what it was like', said she, flinging her hair over her shoulder with a toss of her head.

Haycroft smiled.

'They keep you waiting a dreadful time', she continued. 'You stand in a hall and ring a bell, and an angry-eyed porter opens the door a little way and asks your name; then you wait in this dim sort of cavern and hear strange rumblings in the hidden recesses; presently the doors are broken open by some picture-frame which you hope - and fear - is your own; probably five others appear in the same manner, and the sixth happens to be yours; at least I had to wait as long as that yesterday. The cabman was most sympathetic, "They don't know one from t'other Miss" he said, "I've carried beautiful pictures away".'

The clock had struck four and the model was gone; some of the students left at once; others stayed, chatting as they put their things away. Miss Thornely was cleaning her palette.

'That reminds me', said Haycroft. 'What do you think of long engagements?'

Miss Thornely half looked up, bent over her palette again, then turned to her friend with a pleasant smile and said clearly,

'How do you mean?'

Haycroft rather wished his question unasked, but he replied with the least shade of embarrassment.

'Don't you think it unfortunate for people to have to wait - to be engaged, you know, for years before they are married? There are so many things may happen - they may drift apart you know - oh, there are no end of things.'

'Yes, I dare say you're right,' said she quietly, 'I haven't thought of it'

'There seems to me to be something unmanly in a fellow pledging anyone to anything of that sort when he hasn't a penny in the world - and a good many people do that', he said with a ridiculous reiterated nod of his head.

To be accurate and to give you a just idea of the economy of art schools, I must tell you that Miss Thornely slowly wiped her brushes on a piece of paper; this she carefully folded up and dropped into a hole in the floor.

'After all', Haycroft continued, nursing his knee and looking fixedly at the floor, 'It doesn't much matter if we don't realise our ideals in this world - there is always the infinite future', and he looked up with a smile.

'The infinite future,' said she, with the tenderest satirical intonation, 'is not quite so certain and as for ideals, I don't know whether we exactly understand what we mean by them.'

She looked at Haycroft and smiled gravely.

'I fancy,' she continued, 'some of us - some women, for instance - would be embarrassed to find they had two or three ideal husbands when they arrived at the infinite future - or at least the early part of it. I don't think I make myself clear. There is only one perfect ideal conceivable, in which everything good is merged - but that is inconceivably distant and what will happen after is also rather puzzling – meantime, subordinate ideals differ from one another very much and are each very worthy. Moreover the 'infinite future' is itself the haziest guess, so that there is something as unmanly as a long engagement - in putting things off to that uncertain time in the way, which is so much the fashion. There's a long sermon!' she said with a quiet laugh.

'Ah', said Haycroft with a nod, 'I have a much stronger belief in the infinite future - but I see we are agreed about long engagements'.

'Yes, I suppose we are', said Marian looking at him frankly. Haycroft rose to go.

'Can you tell me' said he 'the subjects for the Sketching Club?'

'Mayday, Disturbed and a Pool, I believe', she said, amused at the incongruity.

'Hm' muttered Haycroft after a minutes pause 'I know what I shall do'.

'May I know?' inquired Marian.

'No, it's not good to tell what one's going to do, is it? I don't know - you shall see. Good-bye.'

They shook hands and Haycroft strode through the outer room, where the Antique figures stood, up the steps into the dark anteroom, away through the hall and into the sunny street. That evening he began a sketch for the Sketching Club. He chose the subject, 'Disturbed', and the composition was something like this: it was a sea shore on the left, in the foreground was a figure of Cupid, decrepit and ugly, sternly fitting an arrow to his bow, and though his head was turned away, you were certain there was a look of successful cruelty on his face: a few yards away there were a number of youths and maidens; some still unwounded and unconscious of the presence of the angel of discord, laughed and talked in happy groups; others walked in pairs, one or two wrapped in bliss although the blood trickled from their wounds. The rest, divided, anxious, restless, with outstretched arms and tortured faces: beyond was the sea, and headland after headland clear and blue. When after some days this was finished, it was carefully mounted and on the back was written the following inscription:

Disturbed

'There is no evil angel but love'. Shakespeare.

David Haycroft

But to return to Miss Thornely; she slowly put her colours in her box and carried that and her canvas to their places in the anteroom. There she stood for a minute with her hands clasped so firmly that when she loosened them, the impression of her fingertips left a mark which only slowly erased itself: then an amused smile dawned and brightened in her face, and she said half aloud addressing herself,

'What! a young knave, and beg?

Is there not a war?

Is there not employment?

Does not the King lack subjects?'

The rest of the quote was inaudible…

David could deceive himself no longer; he was certainly in love. At last he found himself in that pitiful state, which he had been at great pains to avoid; and he had arrived there by no sudden and alarming descent, but by a circuitous and rather pleasant pathway.

But the consequences were serious, for he was still dependant on a generous uncle, a sincere conventional churchman, a church-warden I believe. There was already difference of opinion enough between them. David had come to the conclusion that 'nature is the basis of things in general' (which the intelligent reader will at once see is a truism) and was under the impression that he might wear whatever hat he thought would suit him best and hold whatever opinion seemed truest to him; his uncle on the other hand consid-ered his nephew in a dangerous state, full of unsound views and re-sented it as a personal slight; for one's nephew to disagree with one is clearly as much as for one's nephew to call one a fool; so that this was not a time for David to venture on anything so fatally impru-dent as an engagement.

But indeed this love was a very disturbing matter. He was full of high ambitions and vague schemes for the general good; he thought he had long ago made up his mind that love was not for him, that setting aside his poverty, he could not serve two masters, Love & Art. No doubt in any ideal state those two Gods, as most Gods are, were one; but not so in these present troubled conditions of being. He foresaw a married life threatened with numberless fail-ures and vexations, hope after hope being stifled for want of free breath; on the other hand there was just a chance that it might prove the very finest thing possible and be the buoyant dancing wave which should lift him higher than his vaguest hopes. It is these rare possibilities chiming with our desires which so often give us pause even when we see a wise course clearly marked before us: for when David had made up his mind that he could, would, must think of Marian, 'only as a friend', the pleasant doubt suggested itself that perhaps indeed Marian rather liked him, in which case of course he could by no means take action which should hurt her. Immediately a picture of sad, heartsick Marian pining for his stifled love was chased away by a vision of two figures with locked hands and lam-bent eyes silently inter-vowing everything that was good. But al-ways at the end of such reveries he rose with a prolonged shake of the head and a conviction that marriage was not his course, which he expressed aloud to keep up his courage.

Well, a few days after the sketches were sent in for inspection, David called at the school to see them. Need I tell you that he hoped to see his 'friend', Miss Thornely? He flung his hat on a bench in the dark anteroom, and walked into the parlour, a dim room hung with armour and other curiosities and made comfortable with old furniture. Outside in the street was an organ playing one of those barren jumbles of sound, which is repeated day after day, as though it were the very tune, until suddenly with its fellows it is cleared away and another set as dull takes the place of them. Within an armchair by the fireside sat Marian, pale and beautiful, her head encircled with its masses of loose dusky hair. There was certainly nothing commonplace about this young lady; here at least was an ideal realised, thought David.

'How fine your sketch is Mr. Haycroft', said Marian after they had greeted one another.

'Do you really like it? I am very glad', said David, hurriedly turning over the sketches in the portfolio.

Immediately the one in question was produced and criticized with great animation. Then the conversation branched off into many art subjects full of interest to them, while the other sketches were looked at together, getting now and then a parenthetical word of criticism. Presently David's sketch was set up again. David demurred.

'It's very beautiful', said Marian incisively, 'it is full of pathos; that piece is fine but why', she turned toward him. 'Why do you make love so unworthy a thing? Why do you picture those who are still unwounded as much happier than the others?'

'It is so'

'I don't agree with you; love is only fearful to those who are afraid'.

'But who with his eyes open can do anything else but be afraid?' said David. 'Remember my cousin's case, who at the end of a four years engagement was told he could only be looked on as a 'friend'; or Benson and Drew and Miss Kingsdale, all excellent people - who are probably at cross purposes to this very time; or of Mathews who has married a pretty little fool, and has magnanimously given up every pursuit but money getting; or of Mrs. Wing who went gaily on her wedding tour to Florence and came back solitary six weeks after. No, no, *there is no evil angel but love*.

They were silent a little time. David had a strong impulse to state his own case as a convincing instance; this might have proved too effective, so he thought of it instead.

'I do not like you to say that', Marian answered presently. 'It is cynical; this is too tempestuous, it isn't true', she indicated his sketch with a sweep of her hand.

'You are not one of these happy people who are still unconscious of the evil angel, and yet I don't think you can know what love really is. It is terrible only when feared'.

Her eyes flashed on him for a second and then looked downwards, her head moving with a slight action of scorn. She could say no less: she would certainly not say more.

'I know it, I know it', said David hurriedly, wondering where this woman had learned her lesson in love that she should teach him.

'I know well it is the finest thing there is, and really I don't care two straws for any scruples. But I know this too, that like all best things it cuts pretty deep'.

She should know that he had as good an ideal and as true an experience as she. If she liked someone else, as who could tell whether she did or no, he, poor fool, least of all, he was safe enough from any 'long engagement' and might unburden his mind with bitterness if he liked; certainly without fear. He rapidly turned over half the leaves of a Bible, which lay, at his elbow. Marian was blindly looking at his sketch; she too was aware now of her half-admission. It was miserable if he thought she had learned her lesson of any but him, though truly she had learned much of this matter. Have we not all? from many slight experiences dead and buried; somehow he must be let to know. But perhaps he did not care for her; but perhaps he did and was poor and thought long engagements unmanly. What did it matter, anything was better than less than nothing.

She turned to look at him, hoping something might happen to prevent her from deciding for herself. David looked up too and saw her lovely face, her lovely hair, her parted lips, and her puzzled beautiful eyes.

'Oh, you are too beautiful', he muttered almost rudely turning away again, while the thought of his excellent uncle, his poverty, his career, and heaven knows what else beside flashed through his mind.

His rudeness cost him the loss of what was much more beautiful though, for he did not see the puzzled expression slowly melt, and dawn into a smile of perfect confidence; he knew nothing till he felt the slightest touch and heard strange words fall slowly one by one like beautiful music.

'David, I think we have a strong regard for one another'.

He looked up with light in his eyes and saw her calm and beautiful; their hands were clasped and they were somehow directly after, even locked in a close embrace, their hair mingling, and their language such as has been known from a very early date.

Deconstructing the Story

The story was probably autobiographical. It most likely took place in the autumn of 1878, which was the only occasion in which Caroline was at Heatherley's and Tom was at the Slade. The names of the main characters were significant. Marian was a favoured name, given to their daughter, Phyllis Marian Gotch; Thornely described the prickly nature of the heroine. The name Haycroft was particularly apt, describing Tom's mop of golden hair that Stanhope Forbes was to liken to 'an unmade bed'.

Heatherley's Art School

The description of the studio in which Marian Thornely worked was clearly a description of Heatherley's Art School. Heatherley's was in Newman Street, just off Oxford Street near Tottenham Court Road. It was a private school and students paid a fee; there was no entrance examination and women were admitted on equal terms with men. It was run on the lines of the Paris studios, with few restrictions or conditions. [7] Tom Gotch described this as 'the liberty to paint, to draw hands or do what you will'. [8]

The school was built looking over a garden. Inside, the costume models sat in the rear portion of the studio while the nude models were posed at the extreme end, divided off by a screen and

7. Heatherley's: a hundred years of a famous art school', Heatherley's, 1945 (Tate Archive).

8. Letter from T. C. Gotch to Jane Ross, 18th November 1877.

curtains. This was 'the life room' that David Haycroft entered by 'lifting that part of the curtain, which hung across the doorway, and dropping it behind him'. Most of the art school was crammed with antiques and other objects that Heatherley collected. It was 'a wilderness of Flemish tapestry, Venetian mirrors, armour, tortoiseshell cabinets from Spain, pictures in gilded frames and chairs upholstered in tattered brocade.' [9]

This was one of its attractions and quite well established artists would join the school for short periods in order to use its models and its eclectic collection of objects to make studies for larger paintings. This sounds very like the parlour in which David Haycroft found Marian Thornely, 'a dim room hung with armour and other curiosities'.

A Sketch Club is also mentioned in the story. Heatherley's Sketch Club was a well-established institution that was open to current and past students of Heatherley's. It ran a monthly competition in which sketches were submitted on a series of topics decided by Heatherley. Tom was a member of this club throughout his time as an art student and after he had left Heatherley's he continued to send sketches to the club, which Jane Ross often collected for him because she lived nearby. [10] The best sketches were awarded prizes, which were chosen on the basis of a voting system in which each club member cast a vote. Tom was still submitting sketches when he was a student at the Slade.

Dating the Story

The story makes reference to David Haycroft's dependence 'on a generous uncle, a sincere conventional churchman' and a difference of opinion between them. David believed 'he might wear whatever hat he thought would suit him best and hold whatever opinion seemed truest to him'. On the other hand his uncle considered his nephew 'in a dangerous state, full of unsound views and resented it as a personal slight'.

The true story was that on 21st June 1878 Tom had an unpleasant interview with his Uncle, Sam Gale, who was his mother's brother and the husband of Fanny Hepburn. The Hepburn relations from Clapham (jokingly referred to as Park Village) had taken in

---

9. Spanton, 1864.

10. Letter from Jane Ross to T. C. Gotch, 19th September 1878.

the family when Tom's father was bankrupted in 1857. Tom had been a son in this family and was especially fond of his Aunt Fanny. The row was ostensibly about Uncle Sam's displeasure at the way in which Tom dressed. For Tom to have enshrined this incident in his story suggests that the criticism of his relatives was deeply felt by a young man whose attractive disposition and good looks had always made him a favourite.

> The incident of 'the green hat' puts the most likely date of the story as the autumn of 1878, soon after the event took place; however the reference in the story to 'getting one's pictures from the Academy' suggests a date in March or April when artists had to pick up the pictures that had been rejected for the summer exhibition. Tom submitted pictures which were rejected in 1878 and 1879.

After the row, Tom confided in his brother Alfred who was in London. Realising how upset he was, Alfred sent Tom a letter immediately after their meeting. Alfred was understanding but practical and advised Tom not to alienate the family who should be regarded as possible clients in the future. Under the circumstances the wisest thing was for Tom to give way and at least take some care over his dress before issuing into well-known haunts, where he was likely to run into his relations. [11] Henry heard about the row some time later and although sympathetic, admonished Tom for his lack of courtesy.

> 'People who do us kindnesses have a certain right to be considered', wrote Henry, 'and it would not usually be thought … an offensive thing if they desire us to frequent their society in such attire as the world agrees for the present to regard as distinctive to gentlemen. Again surely there is a want of due perception on both sides when one man says to another "You certainly are my sister's son but I really can't speak to you if you wear a green hat" and the other bids his censor to consider what a green hat is amid the eternities and to amend his life, bringing his practice nearer to his profession …' [12]

On the whole, said Henry, Tom had probably done well to make his views public so that he was no longer walking amongst his relations

---

11. Letter from J. A. Gotch to T. C. Gotch, 21st June 1878 .

12. Letter from H. G. Gotch to T. C. Gotch, 15th July 1878.

'a wolf in sheep's clothing'. 'I for the nonce', ended Henry jocularly, 'must say your depravity does not come up to what your seriousness would lead me to expect.'

Although the row was directed at the way that Tom dressed in public, this was only the tip of the iceberg. Probably the London of 1878 was no different from the London of other times in that it was the melting pot of new ideas. 'This was a time when socialism and free-thinking were struggling against entrenched Victorian conformity.' [13] Art students debated the ideas of the more radical preachers as enthusiastically as they debated the doings of the politicians.

Tom was sufficiently interested in the preachers to include 'all Haweis's works' in the imaginary list of books to be read by him that he described in a letter to Jane Ross. [14] Haweis was a popular preacher and significant enough for Jacomb Hood to include a reference to him in his autobiography, nearly 50 years later. Apparently James McNeill Whistler had lived in one of the small houses in Cheyne Walk, close to the Haweises. Jacomb Hood had received an invitation from Whistler to a luncheon, and Whistler had written in the corner of the card as an additional attraction, *'To see the Haweises go out on tricycles'*. [15]

During the spring and summer of 1878 Tom and his brother Alfred were frequent visitors to the chapel in Holloway where Mark Wilks preached his sermons. Mark Wilks was considered to be a kind of bridge, which generally conducted people from orthodoxy to South Place. Talk of the notorious South Place Chapel would have filled Tom's orthodox, capitalist, Baptist, Victorian middle class relations with the utmost horror; just as (quite separately) the Tuke family had similar feelings when Willie Tuke became an ardent radical and republican and went to hear the Positivists and Moncure Conway on a Sunday rather than accompanying the family to hear a good Quaker preacher. [16]

Tom's relatives were upset by his apparent embracement of these new ideas. They might also have been concerned about his

13. Price, 2001:1

14. Letter from T. C. Gotch to Jane Ross, 18th November 1877.

15. Jacomb-Hood, 1925.

16. Sainsbury, 1933:31.

London life style and the company he kept. Was it to this that Alfred referred in his letter? He wrote:

> 'They apparently don't mind your risking your soul • as they must consider you are doing if they thoroughly believe their own doctrines, and are at all aware of your proclivities • because I suppose you can do that in private, but they make a dead stand against something which is of much smaller importance, but is attended with public inconvenience to their prejudices.' [17]

Could these 'proclivities' have been of a sexual nature? Tom was fond of the ladies and also kept company with men whose inclinations were most certainly homosexual. I think it most likely that Tom's proclivities were his radical ideas and this is what Henry meant by him being a 'wolf in sheep's clothing'.

> Dr. Moncure Daniel Conway was the most radical of the preachers of the time and was the minister at South Place Chapel, London from 1864 to 1897. Conway was born in Virginia in 1832. As a young man he had studied law but later he entered the Wesleyan ministry and became a Unitarian minister at Washington. Conway reputedly had a fine feeling for humanity. His father held slaves in the southern states and when Conway inherited the estates he freed the slaves and became an ardent member of the anti-slavery campaign. When he lost his ministry because of his views on slavery he came to London. South Place Chapel became a popular centre for young men and women with socialist leanings. Conway must have been a wealthy man because as well as being a preacher and an author, he collected pictures and owned paintings by Turner and Rossetti.

Jane Ross

Jane Ross was also a student at Heatherley's in the autumn of 1878. Could Jane Ross have been Marian Thornely? Tom Gotch and Jane Ross discussed 'the infinite future' (which is mentioned in the story) in at least three of their letters. [18] Was this significant to the identity of Marian or did it simply show Tom's interest in the

---

17. Letter from J. A. Gotch to T. C. Gotch, 21st June 1878 .

18. Letters from Jane Ross to T. C. Gotch, 2nd December 1877 and 22 March 1878; letter from T. C. Gotch to Jane Ross, 29th January 1878.

subject? Jane and Tom had been close friends for a number of years. Some of the other students had imagined there was a romantic attachment between them. When Jane Ross had stopped off for a few days in Bruges when Tom was in Antwerp, his friend Rathbone had gleefully remarked 'I suppose Miss Ross is safe in the arms of Gotch'. [19]

FIGURE 3. JANE ROSS (BY HERSELF) CIRCA 1879
SOURCE C. GOTCH, 2000

Tom was drawn to Jane because she was sensitive and intelligent and they shared an interest in literature and books. He spent many pleasant evenings at 82 Gower Street, where Jane lived with her brother. Jane's rooms were often the meeting place for Tom and his friends and both men and women met there without compromising themselves because of the chaperone arrangements put in place by Jane's brother; none the less, some of Jane's letters to Tom could be interpreted as containing barely coded messages about when she was likely to be alone in her lodgings. Jane got to know Tom very well at this time and became so sensitive to his moods that she was able to help him through his self-doubts about his painting. Tom called Jane his 'sister confessor' and she called him her 'penitent'; [20] but I do not think that Jane Ross was Marian Thornely.

19. Letter from J. H. Smith to T. C. Gotch, 27th January 1878.

20. Letters from Jane Ross to T. C. Gotch, 22nd March 1878 ; 30th August 1878.

The Etching Studio

It is not surprising that David Haycroft sought female company at Heatherley's because the teachers at the Slade discouraged romantic attachments between young men and women. Walter Sparrow has left an amusing description of his first day at the Slade:

'The second in command received me, good old Mr Slinger, a tall man, very thin and very ardent, but anxious. His manner was a little flurried, for I was introduced to him by a girl cousin of mine who was among the pupils; and girls caused him much alarm. There were many at the Slade; and as most of them dared to be pretty and original in the midst of boys and young men, poor Mr Slinger's mind was agitated all day long, devising plans to keep Cupid away from art students. He seemed to regard the little imp god as an unlimited company that worked all over the school by means of deputy experts.' [21]

Cupid aside, there was little time for social dallying at the Slade during that first term and Tom spent long hours in the etching studios. Alfonse Legros, the professor had come to England originally to teach etching at South Kensington and his interest meant that the Slade excelled in its promotion of work in this medium. George Percy Jacomb-Hood described how,

'Legros had rigged up the top floor of the building as an etching room, and there, every Saturday, Goulding the master printer attended and some of us started cheerfully on spoiling many copper and zinc plates'. [22]

Tom developed a keen interest in etching and had some success selling his work but he found that it was a lengthy process. David Haycroft's admission that 'we stand about or gossip ... making little half-finished idiotic remarks - precisely like youths trying to kill a wet day,' is a clue to the time when Tom began to form friendships with other Sladers. Etching was Tom's first significant success as an artist and this would have strengthened his relationships with those with whom he shared this success; in fact the friendships he formed at this time with George Percy Jacomb Hood, Joseph Benwell Clark and Henry Scott Tuke, were to last a lifetime.

---

21. Sparrow, 1925:93

22. Jacomb-Hood, 1925:12

Diversions

One important friendship formed by Tom Gotch during those long hours in the etching studios was with Henry Scott Tuke. Harry Tuke had been a student at the Slade for nearly 4 years and was aged 20. He was the second son of liberal minded Quaker parents. Harry's father was a specialist in the treatment of mental disease, but Dr. Tuke had developed tuberculosis and the family had moved to Falmouth where Harry spent part of his childhood. In 1874 the Tukes moved back to London so that Harry's brother Willie could study medicine at University College. [23] There was talk of Harry entering a bank but he was allowed to study art at the Slade instead. He won a three-year scholarship in 1877, thus justifying his parent's decision to support him as an artist and when two of his pictures, 'The Good Samaritan' and an etching of William Strang called 'The Highland Boy' were hung on the line at the RA in 1879, just before his 21st birthday, they had no reason to regret their decision.

Given the remarkable congruence between Tom and Harry's backgrounds, it is not surprising that they became good friends; one from a Baptist family, the other from a Quaker, one from a Banking family, the other having contemplated work in a Bank. Their friendship was consolidated when they decided to go on a sketching holiday together. The Tuke family had rented Meadfoot Lodge, an uncle's house in Torquay and Harry Tuke, his brother Willie and his sister Maria intended to spend part of their summer vacation there. [24]

That summer, Tom was planning to visit Tom and Josephine Hepburn who lived at Hele, Cullompton. Tom Hepburn was Tom's first cousin on his mother's side. Cousin Tom's parents, 'Aunt and Uncle Thomas' were also to be there and a number of other relatives including Tom's Uncle, Dr. Fredrick Gotch and his cousins, Francis (who was a medical student at University College), and Katie (who had married Edward Robinson and had two young children); Tom's brother Alfred was also to be there.

Tom's desire to visit Devon was probably influenced by the fact that Josephine Hepburn's sister Maria Robinson was at Cullompton. Tom and Maria had met in 1878 and had corresponded for

---

23. Price, 2001:2

24. Sainsbury, 1933:33-34

some time, sparking rumours of romance. When Tom wrote to Josephine proposing a visit, the latter's enthusiasm was guarded and she took the opportunity to point out that Maria was now happily engaged to Mr. Arthur Wills of Penzance, who was a 'nice fellow'. She diplomatically suggested that Tom might like to visit later towards the end of the summer, as the house was to be full of other family before then. [25]

It was an ideal opportunity to join Harry Tuke for a sketching holiday and Harry was keen to take Tom to Falmouth where he had spent his boyhood. Tom was also aware that Caroline Yates would be in Newlyn and the two young men planned to visit her. Tom set off for Torquay around 2nd August 1879, following Harry's advice about travel.

> 'The best train to come down by is the 9 am train at Paddington reaching here at 3.33. I will meet you at the station here if you think this train will suit you. I do not wish to bother you with bringing down much extra luggage for me, but I don't see how I am to get on without an easel; if you wouldn't mind I should be very glad if you would buy me one of Roberson's. I fancy they are about 10 or 12 shillings, and slide up something like this [sketch here] with little pegs. Clark had one of the kinds I want. I do not mind much about canvas, but if you are bringing down any you might go to the length of 3/ -to 4/ -for me… I have got … plenty of oils, watercolours, Indian ink and brown ink. I do not want a sketching stool'. [26]

Tom had written to suggest that he bring a bible and a Shakespeare. Harry, who favoured an outdoor approach to life, was not so keen. Reluctantly he suggested that a 'Spenser' was more useful because Jacomb-Hood had come up with a scheme to illustrate a special edition with etchings and he wanted Tom and Harry to participate. Tom was more familiar with Shakespeare than Spenser; he had admitted to Jane Ross that 'a shelf groaning with heavy books' (including Spencer's Faery Queen) awaited him once his art studies were through. [27] In the end Harry persuaded Tom to bring a Spenser and in due course Tom made an etching for an illustrated

---

25. Letter from Josephine Hepburn to T. C. Gotch, 18th July 1879.

26. Letter from H. S. Tuke to T. C. Gotch, 27th July 1879.

27. Letter from T. C. Gotch to Jane Ross, 18th November 1877.

edition of Spenser's Faery Queen; unfortunately nothing ever came of the venture because only Jacomb-Hood and Tom Gotch completed their contributions. [28]

Torquay and Falmouth

Tom arrived in Torquay with immense quantities of stores (which characteristically included an umbrella) and was met by Harry and his sister Maria. They spent a pleasant evening with the family and had a good deal of music thanks to Maria; Willie, Harry's brother favoured them with the one air he had mastered, 'Go to bed, Tom.' [29] Later, when Tom ribbed him about this, Willie said 'How insulting to imply that I had nothing more in stock than 'Go to bed, Tom!' when before I left Torquay I had become a proficient in some three other airs!' [30]

FIGURE 4
HARRY TUKE , SELF PORTRAIT, 1879
SOURCE: SAINSBURY, 1933

Some days after arriving in Torquay, Tom and Harry left for Falmouth on their sketching campaign. Besides sketching, reported Maria Tuke, there was to be much fishing and bathing and looking up of old friends. They went to tea with Lydia Tregelles, an old Quaker lady, who asked many questions about Gotch's family and whether his father approved of his being an artist, and turning to Tuke she asked, 'does thy father quite concur in thy profession?' [31]

Apparently Harry's father had his reservations about his son's life style and pointed

28. Jacomb Hood, 1925:12-13.

29. Letter from H. S. Tuke to T. C. Gotch, 20th July 1879.

30. Letter from W. S. Tuke to T. C. Gotch, 17th December 1879.

31. Sainsbury, 1933:34.

these out to him.

> 'I have sometimes said to you', Harry replied to his father's letter, 'that I think it is a great mistake to keep work, religion and daily life apart, as some people seem to think it necessary to do; they are so dependent on each other that they ought to be moulded together into one simple whole, and I think that a man who does his work badly is just as wrong as one who commits what is generally understood as a moral fault...' [32]

On Sunday 7th September Tom and Harry walked from Falmouth to Newlyn. [33] There they met up with Carrie Burland Yates and her sister Ess. There is little information about how long Carrie had been in Newlyn or why she had ventured there. By this time, the Great Western Railway had completed its extension into Penzance, but although Newlyn was about a mile walk from there along the beach, it was relatively untouched by tourism. Caroline is said to have used the small house directly overlooking the old Newlyn pier as her studio. Although there were other artists painting there at the time, Henry Martin and J. C. Uren, the sight of a woman painting local scenes must have been a novelty. One of Caroline's sketches from this period, 'Newlyn Old Pier and Gwavas Lake' shows the calm water of the harbour, the old pier and the sloping silhouette of the hill behind the town at sunset. [34] There is also a small watercolour by Tom, 'By the Coast Cornwall', signed and dated on the back T. C. Gotch 1879. [35]

It could be that Tom made the sketch for his later etching 'Landscape' while he was in Newlyn. The etching shows a view of pine trees with an artist at her easel and a seated model. One copy of this etching is inscribed *T.C.Gotch to C.B.Y., Hampstead.* [36]

Abraham and Isaac

Tom and Harry left Newlyn on Tuesday 9th September. They caught the train from Penzance to Plymouth and parted company there.

32. Letter from H. S. Tuke to his father, 22nd August 1879 (Sainsbury, 1833:34).

33. Letter from H. S. Tuke to T. C. Gotch, 14th September 1879.

34. Exhibition Catalogue ' Women Artists in Cornwall 1880-1940', Falmouth 1996 (40). Illustrated.

35. Exhibition 'The Rustic Image: Rural Themes in British Painting, 1880-1912', Fine Art Society, November 1979.

36. Hepburn, 1994:11.

Tom headed for Sidmouth, where he was to stay with Tom and Josephine Hepburn. [37] His visit was particularly fruitful and his painting 'Sidmouth' was one of two pictures shown at the Academy in 1880. [38]

From Sidmouth Tom accompanied Josephine to the Hepburn family home at Cullompton in time for the opening of the new Sunday School room on 14th September. Harry Tuke wrote to Tom on the 'lovely Sunday' when the schoolroom was due to be opened and sympathised with him 'shut up in a stuffy schoolroom and listening to verbose speeches'. [39]

But there was more profit in Tom's stay at Cullompton than Tuke might have anticipated. Tom found time to visit an old house at Bradninch with its 'jolly carving', which his brother Alfred had seen previously. Several rooms were panelled and over the chimneypiece were three carved panels: the middle represented Job, covered with knobbly boils; the right hand panel showed Jacob wrestling with an angel wearing 'a pretentiously thick and flowing garment'; the third panel showed Abraham in a 16th century dress about to cut off Isaac's head with a sword, while an angel had seized the point of the sword and was holding it. [40]

Tom was struck with the composition of this panel and made sketches of it. The picture was completed later and executed in grisaille, which is a painting executed in monochrome in a series of greys. *Abraham and Isaac with the Angel* is now part of the permanent collection of the Alfred East Art Gallery in Kettering.

Etching at the Slade

Tom's first public success was when two of his etchings, as well as the 'Goddesses' of Joseph Benwell Clark and etchings by Harry Tuke, were accepted for the prestigious 7th Black & White Exhibition at the Dudley Gallery, [41] which opened to the public on

37. Letters from Josephine Hepburn to T. C. Gotch, 21st August 1879; 6th September 1879.

38. T. C. Gotch pictures at Royal Academy 1880: 'Sidmouth' (903) and 'Study of a Head' (1293).

39. Letter from H. S. Tuke, Torquay to T. C. Gotch, 14th September 1879.

40. Letter from J. A. Gotch to T. C. Gotch, 17th August 1879

41. Letters from J. B. Clark & H. S. Tuke to T. C. Gotch, 18th September 1879 & 17th September 1879.

FIGURE 5
GRISAILLE SKETCH OF ABRAHAM AND ISAAC WITH THE ANGEL, CIRCA 1879
ALFRED EAST GALLERY KETTERING

June 9th 1879. It is likely that one of these etchings was the result of an exercise set by Legros to illustrate a verse of Keats's poem, La Belle Dame Sans Merci. Tom probably made the drawing during his first term at the Slade as he gave a sketch of 'La Belle Dame' to Gertrude Laurie at the end of 1878. [42] Tom's mother was overcome with delight. 'I am truly glad you have something in the Dudley' she wrote. 'Have I seen the two that are received? May it be the beginning of a 'beginning' my boy? [43]

> That year the Black & White Exhibition included 586 sketches and drawings in chalk, charcoal, pen, sepia and Indian ink and etchings and engravings and the like. The critics thought that many of the works were of high merit and none of them were without artistic interest. The exhibition included works by Poynter, Burne-Jones Waterhouse and Whistler. [44]

On 29th June, Tom and his two friends Tuke and Clark were asked to submit proofs of the etchings being shown at the Black & White to Messrs. Dowdeswell, of the Fine Art Gallery in Chancery Lane with a view to business. [45] Fredrick Goulding was instrumental in the success of his students. He printed proofs for the young artists at a cost of 1/- each and when Tom grumbled at the terms, Goulding said that 50% ought to clear all expenses and this would right itself 'une autre fois'. Goulding had a sense of humour, and when Tom confided in him that he was expecting a huge demand, the latter with tongue in cheek replied,

> 'Am glad you have made an arrangement for bringing your great work before the notice of the fickle British Public -accept my best wishes for an immense success - at the same time don't count upon too extensive a brood of chickens. [46]

Despite Goulding's warning, Tom's optimism was justified. In March 1880, he submitted four etchings to the RA and his cousin Charles Whymper asked Tom to bring round a 'copy of your etched

42. Letter from D. Edward Laurie to T. C. Gotch, circa 15th December 1878.

43. Letter from Mary A. Gotch to T. C. Gotch, circa 3rd May 1879.

44. Art Journal, 1879:78

45. Letter from F. Goulding to T. C. Gotch, 29th June 1879.

46. Letter from F. Goulding to T. C. Gotch, 3rd July 1879.

27

boy's head' and 'any of your other etchings that you have to dispose of'. [47]

Tom's etchings were rejected by the RA but he made sales elsewhere because in April, Goulding wrote to say he had taken three 'Keats', four 'Girl on Sea Shore', three 'Repas', and three each of two 'Heads'. This made sixteen proofs, plus the four Tom had for the RA and cost a pound sterling; 'so draw a huge cheque on your banker', wrote Goulding. [48]

FIGURE 6
HEAD OF YOUTH, CIRCA 1880
SOURCE: PRIVATE COLLECTION

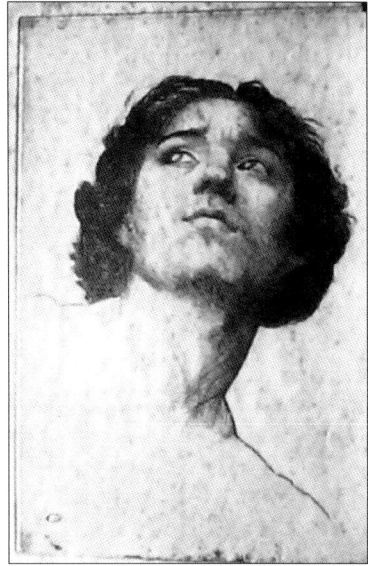

FIGURE 7 HEAD OF MAN, 1880
SOURCE: PRIVATE COLLECTION

'Girl on Sea Shore' depicted the nude figure of a kneeling woman with her head on her hands resting on a rock. 'Repas' was an etching based on the Legros painting, 'Les Repas des Pauvres' and showed a table with two seated figures and one standing figure.

The National Gallery of Victoria, Melbourne has 'La Belle Dame Sans Merci' and four other etchings, which were presented to them by the Felton Bequest in 1939: 'Four

47. Letter from C. Whymper to T. C. Gotch, 9th March 1880

48. Letter from F. Goulding to T. C. Gotch, 24th April 1880

Within the image:

LA BELLE DAME SANS MERCI.

"She took me to her elfin grot
And there she wept and sigh'd full sore,
And there I shut her wild wild eyes
"With kisses four."

KEATS.

FIGURE 8 LA BELLE DAME SANS MERCI, CIRCA 1879
PRIVATE COLLECTION

FIGURE 9 PINE TREES WITH ARTIST PAINTING UNDER AN UMBRELLA, CIRCA 1880
PRIVATE COLLECTION

Heads'; 'Landscape'; 'Head'; and Man's Head. There are a number of etchings in private collections, the largest of which is the Hanbury-Tenison Collection, which contains seven different etchings by T. C. Gotch, including 'Four Heads', 'Boat by the Side of a Lake' and 'Profile Study of a Little Girl', which are thought to have been done in 1877 when Gotch was at Heatherley's.

Art & Life: the debate

While Tom's first year at the Slade was a time of building self-confidence, his second year was a time of experimentation. Many of his older friendships from his days at Heatherley's and Antwerp were maintained through the Shakespeare club. Tom's interest in Shakespeare and the meeting of the Shakespeare reading group continued throughout 1879. This was a context in which he included his family and friends from Kettering: his mother, his brothers and sister, his cousin Frank Berrill and his friend Samuel Dyer. There were also friends from Heatherley's and Antwerp like D. Edward Laurie, Harold Rathbone, Albert Chevallier Tayler, Henry, Walter and Sidney Paget, and the women: Jane Ross, Henrietta Farr, Alma Broadbridge, Miss Naughten, Miss Keo and Miss Hewitt.

Although many of Tom's friends from the Shakespeare group became involved in other circles, none of Tom's new friends became involved in the Shakespeare group with the exception of Caroline Burland Yates.

The Pioneers

By far the most important circle of new friends formed during Tom's second year at the Slade began when he returned to London on Wednesday 1st October 1879 in time to attend 'Graham's Introductory' in University College at 3.30 pm. [49] After the lecture he met up with Willie Tuke, Victor Horsley and his cousin Francis Gotch, who were all medical students at University College Hospital in Gower Street, which was close to Heatherley's and to the Slade. They most likely went to Nicholas's eating-house, which was a vegetarian establishment frequented by students. There, the young men discussed the formation of a new club.

---

49. Letter from W. S. Tuke to T. C. Gotch, 23rd September 1879.

Willie Tuke and Victor Horsley had devised the club in the summer of 1879. Willie wrote to Tom and Harry about the club while they were at Falmouth and the idealistic young medical student captivated Tom's imagination. The new social milieu was to be one in which art students met with medical students. The focus of activity was not literary, as it was in the Shakespeare reading club, but sociological. This no doubt reflected the popularity of the new philosophy of positivism, which was bringing a scientific approach to explanations of life and art. A more equitable relationship between men and women was high on the club's agenda although an agreed form of words to frame this aspiration was never found. Tuke and Horsley explained the purpose of the club as to enable 'social intercourse' 'discussion' and 'mutual instruction' between men and women of similar sentiment. This was a delicate area in the conventional mores of late Victorian England and the 'free thought' that the two young men embraced had to be tempered by discrete language if women were to be allowed to join.

The plan was to collect together a nucleus of members (not more than 20) and to hold a preliminary meeting the first week in October. [50] Victor and Willie had written a draft 'prospectus,' which they hoped would ensure a general community of sentiment regarding things in general but not commit members to any definite opinions. There was a clear intention to safeguard individuality and 'free' thought and draw together people who were broadminded and 'non-creedist'. Horsley wrote to Harrington Sainsbury and Henry Paget. Harry was asked to write to Robert Morley, who might bring a sister or two with him; he also wrote to Caroline Yates.

Willie and Victor wanted to give the new club 'a decided social turn' and would have noted the success with which Tom Gotch attracted females to his Shakespeare readings. It was to Tom, with his 'extensive lady acquaintances,' that they looked to for 'a valuable contingent'. Tom was urged to speak to Alma Broadbridge and Emma Ford as well as any of the Slade girls or other persons he thought eligible. This might have been a reference to Jane Ross as Victor Horsley was keen that they should not just have 'gushing young ladies with nice voices, but ladies with nice brains into the bargain'.

---

50. Letters from W. S. Tuke, 28th August 1879; and H. S. Tuke, 10th September 1879.

Tom carried out his tasks with enthusiasm and contacted his women friends to discuss the 'declaration' that Willie and Victor had produced. Emma Ford entered the discussion with her usual vigour, enthusiasm and original ideas. She suggested that Willie's declaration about 'freedom from convention' should be included but with a rider saying that it was not intended to support immoral behaviour. When Tom sent Willie his and Emma's comments, Willie was delighted with Tom's response but dismissed Emma Ford's suggestions as quite 'out of it.' (So much for equality between men and women!). He thought that Tom's letter and enclosure gave,

> '...decided evidence of a 'nice brain' and I strongly approve of the remark about artists getting more intellectual and scientific influence; though I quite agree with you in thinking the influence should be reciprocal.' [51]

From the start the club had an agenda of facilitating interaction between members of the opposite sex. Presumably there were few female students in medical school, which might have been a significant factor behind the scheme. This interpretation is supported by a letter that Victor Horsley sent to Tom in November in which he asked Tom to arrange an introduction to 'a family in whom the tendency to produce members of the same sex is well marked'. [52] Did the club promoted marriage? Marriages were made between members and their friends and siblings: Henry Paget married Henrietta Farr, Tom Gotch married Caroline Yates, Victor Horsley's sister Rosamund married Francis Gotch; Maria Tuke married Harrington Sainsbury and Charles Gogin married Alma Broadbridge.

The Naïve Willie

The naïve Willie was less successful himself. His first attempt to persuade a woman to join the club ended in disaster. His target was Jessie Crosfield, whom he admired. His plan was to prepare the ground by getting a family friend, one Hattie, to explain the purpose of the club. Unfortunately, Hattie was herself severely shocked when Willie proceeded to explain his views about free love to her! There is no record of what he said, but his later letter to Tom, outlining his views about male-female relations would have been much

---

51. Letter from W. S. Tuke to T. C. Gotch, dated 23rd September 1879.

52. Letter from Victor Horsley, 20th November 1879.

too progressive for most young women of that era.

> 'A further difficulty in the way of solving the problem of man-and-woman is this', argued Willie, 'that sexual desire is by no means in proportion to affection, or vice versa; indeed for a long time at any rate; intellectual intercourse and friendship rather expel the other; and not only so but the female qualities which are calculated to make a nice bed-fellow (excuse plain language) are by no means those which necessarily make an agreeable friend and companion. This divergence involves a most awkward mal-adjustment, and points in rather an unexpected direction.' [53]

In the event, Hattie did not prepare Jessie for Willie's visit and when he called on Miss Crosfield to ask her 'to pioneer', she was alone and not expecting him. Later, she declared that she would never be left alone with him again. The club did have idealistic principles to do with personal freedom also and as Willie, who was diagnosed with consumption, slowly became an invalid and viewed things at a distance, his desire for female company was overshadowed by his desire for an ideal society based on free thought. His practical interest became an intellectual and idealized interest. In fact the issue of male/female relations was never solved and there were recurring disagreements on the wording of the club's 'object'.

The club itself never received a formal name; Jane Ross called it 'the nameless club', while Willie dubbed it 'the anonymous club'. [54] Willie Tuke's illness and absence from the early club meetings was a

FIGURE 10 WILLIAM SAMUEL TUKE, 1878
SOURCE: SAINSBURY, 1933

---

53. Letter from W. S. Tuke to T. C. Gotch, dated 17th December 1879.

54. Letters from Jane Ross, 24th November 1879; and W. S. Tuke, 17th December 1879.

factor in preventing its naming. His friends knew that getting the right name was so important to Willie; he wanted a name for the club that suggested they were 'searching' for a way rather than 'pointing out' a way.[55] 'Although they spoke of themselves as pioneers', wrote Maria Tuke, 'the club never had a name, as none could ever be found sufficiently expressive of its breadth of view and brilliancy of intellect. [56]

The club had its first meeting on Tuesday 7th October. By the end of that month it had elected a president, Victor Horsley, and a secretary, Thomas Cooper Gotch; the members had agreed a set of laws and they had determined a programme of events in which individual members were to make presentations on various topics. The membership of the club included Horsley, the two Tukes, Tom Gotch, Tom's cousin Francis Gotch, William Thompson, Ernest Wedmore, Ernest Radford, De Courcey Skeete, Mrs. Urquhart, Esther and Carrie Yates, Alma Broadbridge, Edith and Gertrude (Bo) Santley, Emily Ford, Mary Sargeant, and Harrington and Gertrude Sainsbury. [57]

William Tuke was taken ill soon after the first meeting of the new club and was sent abroad to convalesce at the Hotel Beau-Rivage in Menton, France with his mother and sister Maria. From there he sent Tom a letter of resignation from the club 'in case the keeping of my name among the list of members of the Club should exclude any other desirable person from becoming a member'. It is unlikely that the resignation was accepted and Willie's friends and brother kept him closely informed. [58]

The programme of events in which individual members were to make presentations on various topics was quite formal and entailed writing a paper and reading it aloud to the other members. When the list of topics for the autumn term was circulated, it became clear that very few of the women were willing to read a paper. Willie thought that feminine garrulity did not extend to writing, and he suggested that Tom should persuade some of the girls to do so. Tom was obviously unsuccessful with Jane Ross who refused to

55. Letter from W. S. Tuke, 23rd September 1879.

56. Sainsbury, 1933: 35-36.

57. Op cit

58. Letter from W. S. Tuke to T. C. Gotch, 30th October 1879

join the club, saying that 'to have to write a paper, and then still worse, to have to read it aloud' sounded simply awful;[59] but he had more success with others because both Emily Ford and Edith Santley made presentations before Christmas.

Willie sent Tom a paper from France for him to read out entitled, 'The aesthetic element in science'.

'I expect neither the artistic nor the scientific spirits in the Club will agree with my essay: I shall be assaulted from all sides. I wish I could take part in the discussion.' [60]

The club also held social evenings and debated current issues and radical ideas. On November 4th Victor Horsley presented a short paper outlining the club's objects. After a hesitant start a lively debate ensued which led to everyone agreeing that members should 'suggest things that wanted reforming, which might be discussed in detail at future meetings'. [61] One suggestion was that members should drop all conventional titles, which even Tom Gotch thought rather drastic.

'Wouldn't Miss Ross feel a thrill of horror at this', he wrote to Miss Broadbridge, 'three of the most promising ladies of the Slade school, Miss Ford, Miss Sargeant and Miss Rosenberg, call themselves by their surnames?' [62]

By the end of its first term of operation, Tom was delighted with the success of the club and his letters to friends contained glowing reports, which gave them a 'peep' into the 'unconstrained intercourse' of the male and female members on club evenings. [63]

Maybe Tom's view was coloured by his romantic adventures of this time because all club members did not share it and William Thompson for one described the 'discussing evenings' as awful failures and suggested that the club would do well to invite visitors if attendance was going to be poor. Another criticism came from Isabel Wedmore. She had attended two meetings and been disappointed at the lack of discussion after Emma Ford's paper. [64]

59. Letter from Jane Ross to T. C. Gotch, 24th November 1879.

60. Letter from W. S. Tuke to T. C. Gotch, 17th December 1879.

61. Letter from H. S. Tuke to W. S. Tuke, 9th November 1879 (Sainsbury, 1933:36).

62. Sainsbury, 1933: 38.

63. Letter from D. Edward Laurie to T. C. Gotch, circa 2nd December 1879.

64. Letter from W.S.Tuke to T. C. Gotch, 17th December 1879.

Thompson was becoming the bane of Tom's otherwise happy life as club secretary. One amusing incident, in which Thompson was the prime mover, was the direct result of the kindness of Tom, Harry and Joseph in allowing club meetings to be held in their studio. Although they had put considerable effort into making Paget's studio habitable at the beginning of their tenure, it probably lacked regular attention. At one meeting, Mrs. Urquhart, announced in a loud voice (which Tom ignored) that there was something that destroyed most of her pleasure in listening to the paper. Later, William Thompson told Tom that he had asked her what was the matter.

> 'She, describing them by a euphemism, which I trust I shall never hear a lady make use of again', explained Thompson, 'told me that whenever she came to the studio she was attacked by fleas. I had not the slightest idea that she meant this at first but it gradually dawned upon me and then I was flabbergasted.' [65]

A number of papers were presented at the club in the spring term. Tom, who always took his responsibilities seriously, had circulated a programme of talks before Christmas. Victor Horsley's topic 'Clothes', provoked a lot of amusement amongst his friends. Ironically, it probably never came off because as the date for its presentation drew closer, Victor received a great shock.

> 'The wind has completely been taken out of my sails by Dr. B. N. Richardson at the Royal Institution the other night,' he explained to Tom. 'Of course it really only expresses the truth of the facts but as his headings were mine I should read and apparently act the part of a plagiarist to perfection. In fact the case is so very strong that I object strongly to reading my effusion under the above circumstances. Kindly mention this to the Committee, and let us consult what can or should be done.' [66]

On the other hand, Tom's paper on 'Life, an Art' went off splendidly. Harry wrote an amusing account for Willie.

> 'Tom Gotch's paper, 'Life, an Art,' came off and afforded a most entertaining debate. Very few understood what he meant, especially those of your gang, (the scientific ones) but of course this did not deter them from making elaborate speeches, all at-

65. Letter from J. W. Thompson to T. C. Gotch, circa December 10th 1879.

66. Letter from V. Horsley, 1st March 1880.

tacking poor Thomas, tho', of course, he did not care for what
they said. Skeete began the debate, and after making one or two
very just criticisms got into a muddle and came to a premature
end. Parkyn came next with a very clear and well-spoken
speech, but as he quite misunderstood TCG it was not much to
the point. Horsley of course trotted out his automata, which was
very diverting to some members. However, they all compli-
mented T.C.G on the 'neat phraseology,' etc., of his essay and
Miss Broadbridge supported him, which he would value more
than the objections of the others. He was also much consoled
by my grand speech at the end, when the President asked us all
round if we had anything to say. I said 'nothing except that I
agree almost entirely with Tom Gotch's paper,' which appeared
to amuse them all very much...' [67]

In fact, Tom's paper was particularly interesting because it presented a criticism of the scientific arguments favoured by the medical students and proposed an alternative to positivism that later gen-
erations of sociologists have called an interpretive paradigm. (The
manuscript of this paper is in the Shears archive.)

Monseigneur Love

Was the story of the Long Engagement literally true or was it
written retrospectively to celebrate Tom Gotch's life-long commitment to Caroline? Could it have been the 'little tale' of Tom's that
Jane Ross gave Miss Naughten to read in August 1879 and was
thought to be 'very French novelish'. [68] If it was this tale and it was
about Caroline, what explanation is there for Tom's subsequent er-
ratic romantic behaviour? If there was a romantic relationship between Caroline and Tom from autumn 1878 to spring 1881 it was
carefully hidden from their friends. I am sure that there was a relationship, and it peeps from behind the better documented events.
For example, once Tom's friend Charles Gogin heard that Tom and
Carrie were to be married, he remembered that they had spent a
good deal of time together at the Slade.

'I seem to remember', wrote Gogin, 'that little friendly criticisms of her were more frequently and strongly hinted at by a

67. H. S. Tuke to W. S. Tuke, February 1st 1880. (Sainsbury, 1933:33-44).

68. Letter from Jane Ross to T. C. Gotch, 23rd August 1879 .

FIGURE 11 MONSEIGNEUR LOVE, 1880
HANBURY-TENISON COLLECTION

male Slade student I once knew than by myself. At that time he
saw a great deal more of her than I did and of course was a better authority.' [69]

Does Tom's picture, Monseigneur Love provide any clues to the
situation? Tom started working on the picture which was to be submitted to the Academy for the summer exhibition before Christmas
1879. It was his practice to test out his ideas for large paintings with
his friends and seek their reaction to them. For example, he explained the picture to Willie Tuke and the latter's amused response
was to hope that the execution of the picture would live up to the
design. [70]

How closely was Caroline involved in the discussions about
Monseigneur Love? The picture shows a man with a bow and a
woman holding an arrow which has been plucked either from her

---

69. Letter from C. Gogin to T. C. Gotch, 15th May 1881.

70. Letter from W.S.Tuke to T. C. Gotch, 17th December 1879.

breast or from the man's quiver. Both figures are silhouetted against a vivid sky. Tom Gotch called this painting his 'first picture' [71] as earlier oil paintings were all portraits.

The subject matter of this work could have been a fragment from David Haycroft's sketch 'Disturbed', that was submitted to the sketch club competition at Heatherley's and prompted Marian Thornely to say that he had 'made love so unworthy a thing' and had pictured 'those who are still unwounded as much happier than others'.

Was the picture for Marian Thornely? Did Tom Gotch intend to make love 'so unworthy a thing'?

David Haycroft's visualisation of his relationship with Marian Thornely was of 'two figures with locked hands and lambent eyes silently inter-vowing everything that was good'. 'Monseigneur Love' is an allegorical painting depicting Cupid with a quiver of arrows slung across his naked back and a young woman scantily dressed in classical attire. The hands of the two young people do not touch as the woman holds an arrow and clutches her breast. Cupid has his back towards the viewer but the woman's face is clear as she gazes at the young man with lambent eyes.

The symbolism of the painting is ambiguous. If the woman plucks the arrow from the quiver, the presumption is that she has chosen to be smitten; if she plucks the arrow from her breast, presumably the young man has chosen to wound her. When Tom Gotch

---

Monseigneur Love

The painting was executed in London between January and March 1880. It was a large oil painting measuring 77 x 99 cm, signed and dated 1880. The RA rejected the painting but it was shown at the Liverpool Autumn Exhibition in 1880 (411) and at the Albert Hall, London in 1882. In June 1883 the painting was put into a sale with a reserve of £2 and sold for £12. In 1901 Tom had a letter from the owner Mr Gilbert of Ipswich, inquiring as to the subject and the title of the work. Rezelman [72] says that at this time Tom Gotch renamed the picture, 'Diana and Actaeon'. In 1976, Bonham's sold it for £300 as 'Mythological Figure Subject'. By 1990 it was in the Phillips sale with an estimated price of £12,000 - £15,000.

---

71. T. C. Gotch's handwritten list of works, Philip Saunders (C86).

72. Rezelman, 1984:204.

was painting this picture Harry Tuke was romantically smitten with Edith Santley and there was rumour of a romance between Tom Gotch and Bo Santley; all four were members of the notorious club! Given its ambiguity, could the painting have contributed to Samuel Butler's anger at Tom's possible role in promoting the romance between Edith and Harry?

Santley and his daughters

Mr. Charles Santley, an eminent baritone, enrolled at the Slade in the autumn of 1879. Santley probably made this decision in order to chaperone his two daughters, Gertrude (Bo) and Edith, who were already studying there. Gertrude and Edith were both members of 'the club'. Tom and Harry became great favourites of the Santley family. The two young men had acquired a piano for their studio and played duets together and Mr Santley gave Harry and Tom singing lessons 'out of pure friendship'. Harry was particularly enthralled with Edith Santley and her rendering of Gounod's *'Oh that we two were Maying'*. [73] Carrie Yates also had a fine voice and took part in the musical entertainments. Harry Tuke's painting of Gertrude and Edith Santley with Carrie Yates, shows the three young women singing, Edith on the right with provocatively parted lips. The painting is a rich, dark, oils on canvas, measuring 66 x 96 cm. It was commissioned by Mrs Santley and hung in the RA in 1880; it is now part of the collection of York Art Gallery. [74]

Inevitably, perhaps, the friendships escalated into romantic flirtations in which Harry Tuke courted Edith Santley and Tom Gotch courted Gertrude Santley. How could this have happened given the sentiment found in 'A Long Engagement'?

The first indication that there was romance in the air came just before Christmas 1879. A musical evening marked the end of the club's first term. It was a symbolic birthday party. The young people deserted the flea-ridden studio and were welcomed into the comfortable Santley house at St John's Wood. Tom, Harry and Joseph Benwell Clark were certainly at the party and it would have been inconceivable if Carrie and Esther Yates, who lived in nearby Warwick Road were not there. Victor Horsley and other members of the

---

73. Sainsbury, 1933:33-44.

74. Price, 2001:3

club would also have been present. Joseph Benwell Clark was the
only person to record the event.

'That was a funny incident about the music', wrote Clark, 'I
can't help laughing when I think about it, now. I wondered to
see you take it when Miss S. offered it to Tuke in the hall as we
were leaving ... I direct this letter to Fitzroy St. where I hope it
will find you struggling with, and overcoming Cupid'. [75]

Does this letter refer to a romantic attachment that Tom had formed
for Bo Santley? If it does, he did not follow things up before Christmas because romance was less important than family commitments.
His brother Henry was due in London to attend the Alpine Club Exhibition and dinner on 18th December. Henry had spent some time in
the Alps that year where he had established new climbing routes. He
was also a keen amateur photographer and some of his photographs
would have been on show at the exhibition. Tom was sure to have
gone to this. On the Sunday before Christmas, Harry called round to
the studio to ask Tom to go ice-skating the next day at the Welsh
Harp, which is the canal reservoir at Hendon. 'They will be there
and have asked me to go home with them in the evening and no
doubt will ask you if you come.' 'They' referred to Edith and
Gertrude (Bosie) Santley. The plan was to get the 10.32 from Kings

Cross and spend the day on the
river, then to go back to the
Santley house. Harry had been
skating the previous day and
had 'a tremendous lark'. The ice
had been thick and strong
though rather uneven. Edith,
Bo. and their brother Mic were
there and also Carrie Yates and
a boy from UCL. They had
hired a sledge (principally for
Miss Yates' benefit) and it had
nearly proved fatal. [76] Tom
could not go because he was
committed to going home on

FIGURE 12

WE ALL SAT OVER THE FIRE FOR HALF AN
HOUR, BO HOLDING MY COAT WHILE I
DRIED MY BREECHES (TUKE LETTER)

---

75. Letter from J. Benwell Clark to T. C. Gotch, December 30th 1879.

76. Note from H. S. Tuke to T. C. Gotch, circa 20th December 1879.

the Monday to help with the production of the Messiah scheduled in Kettering for 23rd December; Harry Tuke called it 'tea fights and entertainments'.

Despite the appalling weather, the day on the Welsh Harp was a great success. Harry had started out early and looking out of the train at Finchley Road he saw his friends all roaring with laughter, under umbrellas, and eating their lunch to pass the time. When they got to Hendon the weather was clearing up; there were only five other people going to skate and no-one to take the money. The ice was covered with half an inch of water, but it was lovely underneath. The girls got their boots and dresses very wet but Harry escaped until about one o'clock when he fell over and was wet through in an instant.

> 'I was such a woeful sight', he reported to Tom, 'that Bosy said she should remember till her dying day. They insisted on my going in and getting dry so we all sat over the fire for half an hour, Bo holding my coat while I dried my breeches. When we got out, Bo fell right on her back, but fortunately had an Ulster so was not much worse.' [77]

Harry wrote this description for Tom's benefit and it is significant that he mentions Bo three times in as many sentences although he himself was obviously enamoured of Edith. Harry continued to dream about Edith Santley throughout the Christmas period.

> 'I received only one Xmas card', wrote Harry 'but ah! who was that one from, do you think. I daresay you can guess; it hoped that 'joy and fair content might crown me through the year', which part she has underlined. I am painting her a New Year's one of some demi-classic people skating, and Cupid coming up behind, rather Gotchine in subject, and a small sequel to it, where they have all fallen into the water, which (with your permission) I may send to Bosy'. [78]

It seems that Harry Tuke and Joseph Benwell Clark believed that Tom was 'struggling with Cupid' and they were keen to cheer Cupid on. Was this a serious romance or was it mischievousness on the part of his friends? There is little other evidence to suggest that Tom was interested in more than a mild flirtation with Bo; perhaps he

---

77. Letter from H. S. Tuke to T. C. Gotch, 28th December 1879.

78. Op cit

played along to give his love-smitten friend Harry, moral support?

Tom also received a letter from Carrie Yates. [79] Apparently Carrie had received a 'jolly little new years card' from Tom. 'I have had none I liked so much, it is just lovely' she said. 'I shall be so glad when the Slade opens to commence work again, what I have been doing here is vile and I feel in the depths of despair about my work … You will no doubt have heard from Mr. Tuke about our last day on the ice', she continued, 'I trust the first thing you do in the New Year will be to get rid of your cough. You have had it quite long enough'.

Was the implication here that Tom had not gone skating on the Monday because he had a cough? Or had he not gone because he had heard about the Saturday skating *and a boy from UCL*? And had Carrie invited the boy from UCL because of Tom's strange behaviour at the Santley house, which was noted by Clark? Could any of these events be significant in the light of 'A Long Engagement'?

One explanation is that Caroline was adamant that her career as a painter should not be compromised by personal relationships. On the other hand Tom yearned for the comfort of a loving relationship. His brother Davis who was radiantly happy with his wife Maud and new baby, Rose Muriel, most probably influenced him. Davis had confided in Tom that,

> 'without them, the home seems scarcely like a home for baby was getting so lively and jolly and so worth seeing every time I came in that I miss her crowing and pretty ways very much'. [80]

Tom's close friend Henry Paget had also just taken the plunge and married Henrietta Farr. His description of married bliss must certainly have touched a chord in the romantic Tom Gotch.

> 'Our domestic felicity is perfect', wrote Paget. 'You would like to see Etta in her white petticoat and looking about 15 (as she always does, when she isn't completely dressed) drumming on my back asking for the matches; and our fire, you would like our wood-fire, with dogs and the bellows, and one big flask of wine holding about 3 quarts and the logs, and our arrangements generally. [81]

79. Letter from Carrie B Yates to T. C. Gotch, 1st January 1880.

80. Letter from Davis Gotch to T. C. Gotch, December 10th 1879

81. Letter from H. M. Paget, Florence to T. C. Gotch, circa. 20th November 1979.

These factors are sufficient explanation for Tom's openness to romance, but he must have been strongly influenced also by the open yearning that his new friends Willie Tuke and Victor Horsley expressed towards women. The relationship between the sexes was at the top of the agenda of liberal discussion amongst the young men. Willie and Victor must have seemed a sharp contrast to Tom's Heatherley's friend J. H. Smith or Samuel Butler, whose attitudes to women were hostile.

Tom Gotch was obviously attractive to women and he was personable and proper enough to instill them (and their chaperones) with the confidence that he would not behave in an ungentlemanly way. Up until the point when the 'Club' came into being the correspondence suggests that Tom formed a number of 'platonic' relationships with women. These were relationships in which the women might have hoped for marriage and where Tom might have unwittingly encouraged these expectations through the literary, philosophical and sociological topics that were discussed. Was this what David Haycroft meant when he spoke about 'that pitiful state, which he had been at great pains to avoid'?

Tom's relationship with Jane Ross was probably the most intimate of his relations with women. Despite the radical philosophies that she adopted in her discussions of literature and art, she was conventional and orthodox in many of her everyday views and practices. She was often self deprecating. She was reticent about joining clubs, even the Shakespeare reading group, although she did in fact take part in this and longed to hear news about it when she was abroad. Still later, she expressed satisfaction that she was not a member of the Club. Jane shied away from 'bonds of union' and told Tom she had an 'extreme objection to being absorbed'. [82]

Jane was obviously aware that Tom had more than a comradely interest in Carrie Yates, and may have been in Caroline's confidence. This may have been the reason for her pointed reference to Caroline in her letter to Tom who was at Falmouth.

> 'When are you coming back? London is horrid, so stay away as
> long as you can - most disinterested advice on my part. Have
> you come across Miss Yates yet? She is at Newlyn, near Pen-

82. Letter from Jane Ross to T. C. Gotch, 2nd December 1877.

zance. I can't remember much about the relative positions of Penzance and Falmouth. They can hardly be very far apart.' [83]

And later:

> 'I was so sorry to miss you yesterday. I had just been talking of you to Miss Yates, with whom I walked hours, and declaring that you could not be in London or you would have come to see me. Such is faith, and its disappointments in this present evil world. She (Miss Y) had had ocular demonstration that you were here, so my remark had little force.' [84]

Friendships with Men

Whatever his romantic inclinations towards women, Tom Gotch maintained a number of close friendships with men. It was natural that he should have an easy relationship with men as he had grown up with three brothers and a large number of male first cousins. Harold Rathbone was a friend from Heatherley's with whom he shared lodgings while at the Slade. In fact, when Tom returned to London from Kettering, where he had spent the last part of his 1879 summer vacation, he was immediately caught up in a major upheaval as he and Rathbone were given notice to leave the lodgings they shared. The landlady had been provoked into declaring that she would not tolerate Rathbone's untidiness any longer and the two were forced to find new lodgings at 25 Montague Place.

> 'I had a good laugh -not a smile -over your account of Mr. Rathbone and the landlady', wrote Jane Ross who was in Italy, 'I am afraid it will not do him any good. Can it be that he is *more* untidy than he used to be? I really sympathize with the landlady, but it was very unpleasant for you, and it is hard to have to leave rooms, which suited you.' [85]

Despite doubts about Harry Tuke's later sexuality, most authors conclude that Tom's friendships with men were not homosexual attachments although Tom Gotch was attractive to other men who may have had homosexual intent. [86]

83. Letter from Jane Ross to T. C. Gotch, 23rd August 1879

84. Letter from Jane Ross, to T. C. Gotch, circa 9th November 1879.

85. Letter from Jane Ross, Rome to T. C. Gotch, 24th November 1879.

86. Gotch, 2000:45-53.

Samuel Butler

One friendship was with Samuel Butler, if not a homosexual certainly a misogynist but one who respected women like Elizabeth Savage, a fellow student with Butler at Heatherley's, who was a dear and life long friend. Butler was the grandson of Dr. Samuel Butler, the famous headmaster of Shrewsbury School. Tom and Butler must have met at Heatherley's in 1876; Butler had been a student there since the late 1860s. Born in 1834, Butler was older than most of the other students. When Tom entered Heatherley's in 1876, Butler must have seemed a successful artist because four of his paintings had been exhibited at RA summer exhibitions between 1869 and 1874 and in 1876 his painting 'Don Quixote' was on show. He seems to have acted as a buffer between the students and the teachers: on the one hand the students saw him as a kind of dominie who kept them in order; on the other hand he was intellectually superior to his teachers so his mockeries and his wit often worked to the other students' advantage. He was a striking figure.

> 'He always wore rough homespun and thick boots, and his hair and beard were cut quite close, the face was short and the complexion ruddy. The eyes could snap and sparkle and they could beam with sympathy. His voice was sweet and low, his laugh quite infectious.' [87]

Tom became friendly with Butler through Henry Paget, who knew that Tom had strong literary ambitions. About this time, Henry Paget was trying to interest Mr. Paul of Kegan Paul, the publishers, in Tom's poetry. [88] Paget thought that Butler could be a useful contact. Butler had published 'A First Year in Canterbury Settlement' in 1863 and the classic, 'Erewhon' in 1872. He also had a prodigious knowledge of philosophy, and a superb command of language. The fact that he played piano music by Handel was another reason for Tom's admiration. In return, Tom Gotch was intellectually motivated, ready to show his admiration and willing to gratify Butler's need to talk about his own paintings. Christopher Gotch has summarized the relationship well:

> 'Samuel Butler ... had a penchant for attractive young men

---

87. Johnston Forbes-Robertson , 1925.

88. Letter from Henry Paget to T. C. Gotch, circa 24th August 1879.

whereas Tom sought encouragement from Butler for his poetry and fiction writing. As it turned out the relationship proved but a moderate success, for Butler ignored Tom's desire for advice on literature … Butler's refusal to acknowledge Tom's efforts at writing probably helped Tom to concentrate upon his painting at this juncture. Irony here too in that Butler wished to be a painter rather than a writer.' [89]

By the time Paget left for Italy, Tom was a frequent visitor at 15 Clifford's Inn where Butler had rooms. Charles Gogin who had lodgings in Euston Rd and a studio in Camden Square was a close friend of Butlers. Tom had met Gogin at Heatherley's. He was a man of remarkable culture and originality, who was said to have had a great influence on the younger men, both artistically and intellectually. He was never widely known as an artist because he would rarely exhibit. [90] It was Charles Gogin from whom Tom Gotch said he had 'learnt more about painting and a painter's outlook than from any other single person.' [91]

FIGURE 13.
CHARLES GOGIN, 1881
SOURCE: SAINSBURY, 1933

Harold Rathbone was on the fringe of this group although Butler, preferred not to include him. 'Most excellent and well beloved Gotch' wrote Butler on one occasion, 'you may come here, Gogin may come here, Paget may come here: Rathbone is not to come here'. [92] At this time Rathbone professed to be a great expert on Italian Art, having been to Italy the previous year. Certainly Henry Paget was enormously impressed with him.

'Rathbone and I have been getting very thick lately … I go into Heatherley's and we do anatomy together. I go into his (I mean your) room and we look at his Italian photographs. I go down to

89. Gotch, 2000:43

90. Sainsbury, 1933:58.

91. Exhibition Catalogue: Children's Portraits & Child Pictures by T. C. Gotch, Laing Gallery 1910.

92. Letter from S. Butler to T. C. Gotch, 18th August 1879.

the riverside and sketch with him, and to clinch it all, we speak
Italian together! Yesterday afternoon … we walked across the
park to the South Kensington Museum, had our chop there, and
spent the evening looking at the Leonardos, Raphaels and Botticellis. Really the Botticellis are very beautiful. This last week,
through Rathbone, I have undergone a considerable enlighten-
ment, much to my own delight and relief, as well as
Rathbone's… Yesterday we looked at all the wonderful Sistine
Chapel, Michael Angelo's. By Jove! I can see ten times the
amount in them that I could a fortnight ago.' [93]

Butler had modelled his own painting on Bellini from early days.
Butler had given Paget a photograph that he had taken of a Bellini
painting that Paget was later to judge as 'awful', saying that the
photograph was 'ever so much better' than the original. Although
Butler was demonstrably anti-marriage, he continued to correspond
with Henry Paget after the latter had married fellow artist Henrietta
Farr, who was a painter of figurative subjects and exhibited at the
Grosvenor Gallery between 1883 and 1884. Writing from Italy, just
after his marriage, the mischievous Henry Paget asked Tom to give
Butler a message,

'I have just asked Etta if I should send her love to him and she
said "Oh yes, for I'm very fond of him, practically though not
theoretically". Tell him that, for I'm sure he will laugh at that.'
[94]

Tom Gotch does not seem to have introduced Butler to Tuke until
after Christmas 1879 and then only at the instigation of Henry
Festing Jones. Was this because Tom felt the need to protect his
young friend Harry or because Butler, who was in Italy during the
summer of 1879, had not returned to London? In fact Harry Tuke
became a regular caller at Clifford's Inn for a number of years although he does not seem to have established the same depth of
friendship with Butler that was established by Tom Gotch.

Last days at the Slade

The 1879-1880 Slade term ended in June. Tom met up with
Carrie Yates on Sunday 11th July, before she and her sister Ess de-

93. Letter from H. M. Paget to T. C. Gotch, circa August 1879.

94. Letter from H. M. Paget to T. C. Gotch, circa November 1879.

parted for Newlyn where they were to spend the summer. [95] From Newlyn, Carrie planned to go with Alma Broadbridge and Jane Ross to Paris to continue their studies. Tom had discussed Paris with Harry Tuke and told him that the women intended moving there.

> 'I think it is very unnecessary for those girls to go to Paris',
> said Harry disapprovingly, 'it will cost them much more and
> there is plenty for them to learn in London yet.' [96]

Harry spent the first few weeks of his holiday at Beaumaris in Wales with his brother Willie and sister Maria. From there he joined the Santley family at Liverpool where they took a steamer to Genoa, and on to Monticello. He was to spend a month sketching in the beautiful mountainous country before they all went home by Lago Maggiore and over the St Gothard.

Butler and Tuke

Harry's decision to go with the Santley family to Italy fuelled the rumour about a possible engagement between him and Edith Santley. Samuel Butler, who had become quite thick with Tuke by this time, wrote to him warning him against marriage.

> 'Don't marry any woman without being so much in love with
> her that you feel you would rather be made into mincemeat than
> not marry her. .... This is how Paget felt towards Miss Farr, and
> the match is and will be a happy one. If you feel like this to-
> wards any woman you can hardly marry her too soon, but any-
> thing short of it is, I believe, one of the gravest crimes of which
> a man can be guilty.' [97]

Harry wrote to Butler from Beaumaris explaining that he and Edith were just good friends. Butler's next letter, sent poste restante to Genoa, showed a change of tack. 'You are evidently not only not in love' but 'you are evidently not one particle in love', he wrote; but something in Harry's letter must have provoked Butler's paranoia about the role that Tom Gotch had played in Harry's romance. Butler was convinced that 'some people', (a reference to the Santleys) had tried hard to ensnare Harry while others, who had taken

---

95. Letter from C. B. Yates to T. C. Gotch, , July 10th 1880.

96. Letter from H. S. Tuke, Beaumaris to T. C. Gotch, 12th July 1880.

97. Letter from Samuel Butler to H. S. Tuke, July 12th 1880 (Sainsbury, 1933:39).

'precious good care to keep out of the mess' (a reference to Tom) had egged Harry on until he had got into a false position. [98]

Harry sent a further note in response to this letter, in which he convinced Butler that there would be no announcement of an engagement with Edith Santley and that his intention was to break away slowly from the relationship. A third letter from Butler, who was at Locarno, suggested that his panic was over but that he still blamed Tom Gotch as the major instigator of the affair.

> 'To me you seem to have been the victim of one of the most unprincipled attempts I remember to have seen tried on upon unsuspecting innocence, and to have been advised by friends who were none the less mischievous for the blindness and stupidity to which their mischief was owing... Don't bring Gotch to see me any more. If you want to see me on your return either come alone, or with Jones or with Paget, but I am tired of Gotch and don't want him any more...' [99]

It is difficult to explain the cause of Butler's sudden seemingly paranoid outburst against Tom Gotch, although the breach between them seems to have been healed later. [100] Maria Tuke thought that Butler was labouring under a complete misapprehension about the people concerned in the affair, as no one was in any sense "unprincipled," and Gotch, whom he blamed, was writing to Harry about the same time, 'my dear boy, do *do* DO close that tragedy.' [101] Unfortunately there is no information about the exact date of this letter or whether it predated the news that Charles Santley had become a Roman Catholic. Harry was already in Beaumaris when Carrie Yates sent a note to Tom with this news.[102] Tom wrote to Harry in Beaumaris immediately. Tuke's response suggested that Tom had advised him not to compromise himself.

> 'Your letter was an immense shock', wrote Harry, 'I hadn't the slightest suspicion that anything of the sort was preparing. Though one often holds that there is no consistent medium between RC and FT, [103] I think the former is the consistency of

98. Letter from Samuel Butler to H. S. Tuke, July 28th 1880 (Sainsbury, 1933:40).

99. Letter from Samuel Butler to H. S. Tuke, August 15, 1880 (Sainsbury, 1933:41-43).

100. Letter from Samuel Butler to T. C. Gotch, circa 5th August 1881

101. Letter from T. C. Gotch to H. S. Tuke, circa August 1881. (Sainsbury, 1933: 43)

102. Letter from C. B. Yates to T. C. Gotch, July 1880.

103. (RC) Roman Catholic and (FT) Free Thought

folly after all, its details, experience has shown to be such gross impositions. I think all these modern sects are a slough that people have to wade through, thank goodness that we have emerged on a tolerably dry piece of land (at least, I hope so). I think the only good thing about Mr. S's affair is that it gives a fixed point for one of the dramatis personae in our tragedy. Still I think it's horrid. I should have thought he would have been the first to hate all their humbugging performances. I begin to suspect that our tragedies are only just developing and we shall regard these blows in future as everyday events; I hope the pleasurable shocks will be on the same scale. As to my conduct in Italy, I will try to behave with an exquisite care. It is really very serious.' [104]

Fortunately, these affairs do not seem to have affected the friendship between Harry Tuke, Tom Gotch and the Santleys; thus there is evidence of a friendly correspondence between Harry Tuke and Edith Santley that continued even after she had married into the Lyttelton family, with Harry spending time with Edith in London as late as 1913. [105] Similarly Tom remained on very friendly terms with the family. He painted a portrait of Charles Santley, which was exhibited at the Marlborough Gallery in 1886 [106] and Charles Santley gave singing letters to Tom's daughter many years later.

The Maria Tuke Saga

Before the 'long engagement' reached its inevitable conclusion there was one more hurdle to be overcome; the Maria Tuke 'affair.' Sometime in August Tom Gotch and his brother Alfred and sister Jessie arrived in Beaumaris to spend part of their summer holiday with Willie and Maria Tuke. Harry had already left for Italy. During this time, 'an intriguing situation developed' and 'apparently Maria Tuke fell in love with Tom Gotch and William Tuke became attached to Jessica Gotch'. [107]

At the time this was no more than a holiday flirtation. Willie, with his usual enthusiasm for the opposite sex constructed a harm-

104. Letter from H. S. Tuke to T. C. Gotch, 12th July 1880.

105. Sainsbury, 1933: 150

106. RBA 1886 (29). Magazine of Art, 1886:353/4.

107. Rezelman 1984:27 Footnote 53.

less fantasy around the more down to earth Jessie and Maria was charmed by the handsome Tom, who became her knight in shining armour, against the seeming tyranny of her parents who would not allow her to go to art school. Unfortunately the situation between Tom and Maria got out of hand; it led to Tom Gotch requesting Dr. Tuke's permission to marry Maria and to Maria most likely falling in love with Tom. Given 'A Long Engagement', how could Tom have put himself into such a position? How did Tom compromise himself in this way when he had seen fit to warn Harry against a similar thing happening with Edith Santley in Italy?

Maria and Tom first met when he visited the Tukes in Torquay in August 1879. Although Tom was charmed by Maria and shared Harry's enthusiasm about her piano playing, he was much more interested in his new friend Harry, and his visit to Carrie Yates in Newlyn. In the few days he was in Torquay he got to know Willie well enough for the beginning of a firm friendship but there was no hint of anything more than a friendly interest in Maria who was 18 at the time.

There is no reason to suppose that Maria and Tom wrote to each other between August 1879 and August 1880 when they met again in Wales. Harry and Willie made passing references to their sister in their letters to Tom. The Tuke brothers most likely talked to Tom about their concern that Maria's aspiration to go to art school was being vetoed by their parents. They would have been proud of their younger sister who showed considerable talent at painting; a talent that eventually led to public recognition. At this time, Maria wanted to go to the Slade. Harry Tuke had already pleaded Maria's case with his father the summer before, but to no avail. Then, Harry had said,

> 'I think a strong argument in favour of her going now is that
> she would be introduced to the nicest circles and warned
> against the noxious ones, though I hope her own good senses
> would be sufficient guide. Besides, Maria can't always be bot-
> tled up, and I should have thought the present would have been
> a very good opportunity for drawing the cork and letting her out
> into the world, where she would be well looked after by her
> father and her brother.' [108]

108. Letter from H. S. Tuke to Dr. Tuke, 22nd August 1879. (Sainsbury, 1933:35.)

Maria's parents were adamant that she could not study art formally although she continued to work at home with the support of Harry.

'Harry has sent me a stock of chalks, charcoal and paper', she wrote to Jessie, 'and I am going to borrow some casts from a school ... here; so I hope I shall get on a little, as even the suggestion that I should attend the Queen's Square School (for Ladies Only) was negatived'. [109]

Tom Gotch recognised Maria's talent and was angry that she was being denied the means to express it. Given his 'well-formed and well-formulated' liberal ideas, the fact that Maria's circumstances were just those that the new club was formed to circumvent, must not have escaped him. The explanation for Tom becoming Maria's champion against the might of the older Tuke family is to be found in his mission-like zeal to live the club's 'objects' in his daily life.

Holiday at Beaumaris

The holiday in Wales marked the start of the 'affair'. According to Maria there were numerous comings and goings by different friends and family; Alfred and Jessie Gotch were in Beaumaris for some of the time; members of the Rheam family were frequent visitors. Willie was seeking a hospital appointment and attending interviews, but using Beaumaris as his base.

In the absence of Harry, who was in Italy, Willie and Tom formed a very close attachment. Tom was delighted with Willie's broad ranging mind. Willie was writing a notice about Bastian that appeared later in the Journal of Mental Science, which he read to

FIGURE 14 MARIA TUKE
SOURCE: SAINSBURY 1933

---

109. Letter from Maria Tuke to Jessie Gotch, 8th October 1880.

Tom 'in the castle of Beaumaris (of sweet memory!)'. [110] They also discussed an essay on feminine intelligence that Willie was just beginning. They shared some of these ideas with their sisters, who were also developing a close friendship, because later Willie sent Spencer's Essay on Education to Jessie, which he thought she would appreciate. Willie and Jessie got on well but there is no indication that Jessie felt more than 'sisterly' affection for Willie. Willie's true feelings are unclear. Later, referring to Mary Wedmore he admitted to Tom that he had a 'susceptible mind' and would 'have to take care not to fall in love with her', but that she was 'not so chef as Jessie'. [111]

FIGURE 15
JESSIE GOTCH BY T. C. GOTCH, 1881
COLLECTION OF CHARLES CLARKE

The holiday in Wales was not completely intellectual and when the sun shone the young people would spend their time bathing, the women using bathing machines. Tom Gotch may have introduced Maria to drawing, painting and sketching outdoors. [112] There is no doubt that the young people developed a degree of intimacy, so that later Maria could send Tom the message that she had found a dish 'even cheffer' than 'thunder and lightning,' which was the name they had given junket and honey. [113] But intimacy is not romance and there is only one episode mentioned in the various letters that could be given a romantic slant and even that may be interpreted as a young girl's romantic yearnings rather than an intentional advance

---

110. Letter from W. S. Tuke to T. C. Gotch, 5th January 1881.

111. Letter from W. S. Tuke to T. C. Gotch, 29th April 1881 .

112. Rezelman 1984:27 Footnote 53.

113. Letter from Maria Tuke to Carrie Yates, 12th November 1880.

on the part of a suitor. Writing to Jessie, Maria confided,

> ' I went up to the reservoir the last day at Beaumaris, alone, to finish my sketch, and saw where each of us had laid the time before by the pressure on the grass, which had not risen since; it was very melancholy but painting cheered me and I wandered about the dear place for some time.' [114]

The occasion may have been very innocent but there is a yearning in Maria's words. That is all that is known for certain about the actual holiday in Beaumaris. The holiday was over by the 20th August.

The Gotches left Beaumaris before the Tukes and Tom arranged to meet Willie at Ambleside at the beginning of September. The records give no clues about where Tom went when he left Beaumaris and two weeks are unaccounted for. Could he have gone to Cornwall to visit Carrie Yates? Tom received a letter from Carrie addressed to him at Beaumaris and dated 16th August. [115] All that is known for certain about this letter is that it contained a detailed description of the Newlyn subjects that Caroline was painting. Tom did two small oil paintings of Miss Caroline Burland Yates, both 20 x 11.5 cm and signed, which their daughter Phyllis said were painted in 1880. One of these paintings is named 'Miss Yates as a Fishergirl'. [116] This suggests that it was painted at the coast. Let us suppose that Tom did visit Carrie and they discussed Maria's situation and she challenged him to put his principles into practice. *Could Miss Thornely have tested 'the young knave' in this way?*

Tennyson's Prince

Towards the end of August, Tom wrote to Mrs Tuke about Maria with disastrous consequences. The exact contents of this letter are unknown. Tom had modern views about women, which would have horrified Mrs Tuke. He had read the work of J. S. Mill and was committed to women's independence. When Tom shared his 'more liberal beliefs' with his brother, Henry had said that most of them were well formed and formulated – that is except for Tom's 'belief of women' which Henry found 'of another character and a

114. Letter from Maria Tuke to Jessie Gotch, 22nd August 1880

115. Letter from C. B. Yates to T. C. Gotch, 16th August 1880. (Rezelman, 1984:317-318).

116. Exhibition 'Artists of the Newlyn School 1880-1900', Newlyn Art Gallery, 1958. 'Miss Caroline Burland Yates (49). Miss Yates as a Fishergirl' (50)

very curious one.' [117] Tom's 'belief of women' was the subject of his correspondence with Maria Robinson, his cousin's sister-in-law, who was 'quite bent on sick nursing'. [118] He had also collaborated with Gertrude Laurie, his friend's sister, on sketches for her pamphlet called, 'The New Magna Charta', which presented an argument for developing a more scientific approach to choosing marriage partners. [119] Tom's beliefs were closely aligned to the objects of the Club, which Willie had formulated. Later, Tom Gotch found a way of expressing these sentiments through his art in pictures like 'My Crown and Sceptre' and 'Holy Motherhood', where he was able to depict real women and children in idealised circumstances and dress.

Mrs Tuke received Tom's letter just before she left Ambleside and showed it to her friends, the Hills. On 1st September Willie wrote telling Tom not to come because of 'another small disaster'.

'There seems to be a feeling roused against you in the authorities of this household, and you must not come on Friday: I am very sorry. Your letter to Mother seems not to have pleased Mrs. Hills, who read it; I have just had a little blow up with Mr. H. on the whole subject. I shall not stay so long as expected ... I shall not have much respect left soon for my Mother or her friends: don't accuse yourself of all this rumpus being your fault; it isn't; it's hers or at least Society's, and you are simply the best and noblest fellow there is. We shall have to fight hard for Maria's freedom, but we shall win in the end; family quarrels are not so sad a spectacle as women in slavery, and the former seem an inevitable part of the struggle to do away with the latter.' [120]

Tom's action was viewed by the older folk as presumptuous. His letter to Mrs Tuke brought no improvement in Maria's situation and probably worsened it. When Tom met the Tuke brothers at Ambleside, they may have discussed the harm that had been done to Maria's cause by the letter. They may have discussed the possibility of marriage as a theoretical solution to Maria's problems.

Harry, whose absence had distanced him from the situation,

117. Letter from H. G. Gotch to T. C. Gotch, 15th July 1878.

118. Letter from Maria Robinson to T. C. Gotch circa 2nd October 1878

119. Letter from Gertrude Laurie to T. C. Gotch, 29th April 1879.

120. Letter from W. S. Tuke to T. C. Gotch, 1st September 1880.

would not have imagined that the theoretical talk of marriage could be taken literally. He tried to play down the situation when he met Maria, treating it jokingly and saying that he looked forward to having a good time, and being quite independent when they were all about 40. Maria seems to have responded in an equally playful way saying that it would be rather hard to wait till then before one had one's fun, although it would be all the more festive when it did come. [121]

In the meantime, nothing so drastic was decided; instead the young men agreed that Tom should try and reduce the damage he had done by writing a more moderately phrased letter to Dr. Tuke, assuring Dr Tuke that his (Tom's) intentions about Maria were quite honourable.

Harry Tuke was in Weston when the letter arrived and 'talked a good deal about the affair' to his father when they travelled back to London together. 'I fancy your letter made a favourable impression on the whole, though he did not say much about it,' reported Harry. It is difficult to fathom Harry's true feelings on the matter and his letter to Tom ended rather enigmatically with a message from R. Fox. 'She wants to know if you have been foolish enough to get engaged yet?' reported Harry. 'She has been lecturing to me on the advantage of having a good father-in-law'. [122]

What was the content of Tom's letter? Was it simply to ask permission to correspond with Maria? Maria certainly wrote to Tom soon after this and probably released him from any commitment he felt towards her, a letter which Maria admitted to Jessie, 'was a mighty job to write'. [123]

At the beginning of October Tom, Willie and Harry were in London, staying with Alfred in Great Coram Street. They were all optimistic about their future: Willie was hopeful of an appointment with Dr. Bacon in Fulbourne, near Cambridge; [124] Harry was to go to Florence, having fallen in love with Italy as a result of his visit with the Santley family; and Tom was to follow Carrie Yates and her friends to Paris where he planned to spend the next three years

121. Letter from Maria Tuke to Jessie Gotch, 8th October 1880.

122. Letter from H. S. Tuke to T. C. Gotch, 19th September 1880

123. Letter from Maria Tuke to Jessie Gotch, 8th October 1880.

124. Letter from H. S. Tuke to T. C. Gotch, 19th September 1880

in the studio of Jean Paul Laurens.

Unfortunately Willie had a haemorrhage and Tom was with him at the time. Tom's first hand experience of Willie's attack was traumatic and probably influenced what followed.

Willie's medical career was at an end and from this time there was a steady decline in his health. His friends and family were aware that the end could come without prior announcement. Willie, confronted by the certainty of his own imminent death made Maria's freedom his main mission in life and to achieve this end he needed Tom as his willing ally. Tom's courtship of Maria had been coaxed into life by Willie's idealism and was to be prolonged because of Willie's worsening condition. Willie's desire to give his sister her freedom was linked to his conception of the 'anonymous' club and its objects. Although many club members thought that the original object suggested 'immoral' relations between men and women, this was certainly not Willie's intention. As he explained later, 'it is surely no worse to talk about sexual selection than to talk about marriage'. [125] This is what he meant when he referred to the club as 'an emancipated group for men and women'. Willie thought that Tom should act in an emancipated way to save Maria!

What of Maria herself? She had written to Tom thanking him for supporting her plan to study art but she had also indicated that she did not expect more than this. She too was drawn into Willie's plan, probably not unwillingly. When Willie was taken back to Weston after his haemorrhage, his sunburn made him look fitter than he actually was but Maria thought he was 'dangerously energetic'.

> 'I am so glad he was where he was when he took ill', she wrote
> to Jessie, 'and that any body so kind as Tom was with him …
> Do you know, the more I know of him (Tom) and see of his
> actions, the more nearly he seems to come up to my ideal man,
> and the more petty and weak he makes me feel myself to be'. [126]

Tom's championing of Maria Tuke was probably a gesture; but he also loved Maria as he did her brothers – not in a sexual way, but because she was young and innocent and 'uncrowned' in the sense that her parents were denying her the opportunity to fulfil her poten-

125. Letter from W. S. Tuke to T. C. Gotch 8th February 1881.

126. Letter from Maria Tuke to Jessie Gotch, 8th October 1880.

tial. Maria probably understood that Tom was motivated from this chivalrous position and that it was propelled by his wish to put into practice the ideals that the dying Willie could not handle. Maria may have genuinely loved Tom for this. The following passage from a letter of Maria's shows a remarkably clear understanding of Tom's character by herself and Willie.

> 'We read aloud a good deal, amongst other things Tennyson's Princess, which I love - better every time I read it too. The Prince seems to me a sort of reflection of Tom, it is most curious; one can see a distinct resemblance in almost every quality. Willie thinks he was rather weak, but I don't at all. [127]

The Move to Paris

When Tom Gotch set off for Paris about the 4th October, he must have been in some despair about Willie's illness. Harry Tuke, who delayed his departure for Italy until he believed that Willie would recover, visited Tom about the 15th October on the way to Florence and was able to reassure him that Willie's condition had stabilised.

Tom's address in Paris was the Rue de Tournon 17. The rooms were spacious and lofty, but they were situated on the top floor and he was unable to get a piano up the narrow staircase. 'What do you do now about practising?' his mother wrote, 'I hope you get some
•   I am afraid it helps to making your life Bohemian, instead of quietly enjoying a practice (sic) at home.' [128] Carrie Yates was living at the Hotel de Paris, which seems to have been a Bohemian establishment. Perhaps Tom practised there and this was the reason for his mother's remark? He did not share his lodgings because none of his young male friends from the Slade were in Paris, although when Harry Tuke joined Laurens in September 1881, Chevallier Tayler, Jacomb Hood and Charles Gogin were also there.

Tom was not uncomfortable in Paris. He had acquired a charcoal stove to heat his rooms (despite Willie's warning that people were often killed in their sleep if there was not proper ventilation) [129] and he had the company of 'the girls' when they were not working

---

127. Letter from Maria Tuke to Jessie Gotch, 8th October 1880.

128. Letter from Mary Ann Gotch to T. C. Gotch, 11th January 1881.

129. Letter from W. S. Tuke to T. C. Gotch, 10.XII.1880.

at the Julien studio. They were all taking singing lessons and Tom was taking French lessons (Carrie spoke good French already).

Adjusting to the new atelier of Jean Paul Laurens was more problematic for Tom than adjusting to life in Paris. The work was challenging, but Laurens was a good teacher and Tom admired his interest and originality in composition. Tom was learning a great deal, but he was played out pretty soon every day. He found that the noise, the heat, the smoke, and the students generally, depressed him beyond measure. [130]

Jean Paul Laurens was a historical painter. He painted subjects of high tragedy. He was elected an honorary member of the RA in 1909 and died in 1923. He was held in high repute as a teacher and attracted many of the up and coming young artists from England to his atelier. Gogin's view was that Laurens was, 'the only sound teacher I have ever heard about. He seems to know so exactly what each man wants and how much to give him. Even when I disagreed with what he said about things, time has always shown me it was my ignorance that was at fault.' [131]

The Saga Continues

There is no doubt that after his haemorrhage Willie came to believe that Tom had committed himself to marriage with Maria. It is quite likely that Willie spoke to Maria and this may have influenced her view. Willie's letters to Tom in Paris were full of the matter. In one that is no longer available, written in late October 1880, Willie wrote,

> "I believe the actual statement Maria made was that she would never marry anyone else. My feeling is that it would be the best thing for some definite arrangement to be made between you next summer, when we must if possible arrange a meeting. Of course, if you are both firm, you have everything in your hands'. [132]

130. Letter from T. C. Gotch to H. S. Tuke, April 1881` (Sainsbury, 1933:55)

131. Charles Gogin, quoted in Sainsbury, 1933:54

132. Letter from W. S. Tuke to T. C. Gotch, late October 1880 (Rezelman, 1984:27 Footnote 53.)

At this time Tom was probably wondering how he could get himself out of the situation but his reserve, and desire to please prevented immediate action. Instead, he threw himself into his work and hoped things would right themselves. By November he was working at Briqueville-sur-Mer, a location of the Laurens atelier and was 'incognito' as far as letters from home were concerned. While he was there Carrie received a letter from Maria Tuke with the news that Willie had had another serious haemorrhage. The situation to those who remained with him seemed 'horribly hopeless' and his mother had moved into his room to watch over him. [133] Maria asked Carrie to pass the news to Tom. At this time Carrie acted as an intermediary, forwarding mail that came to Tom's studio or passing on messages. Although Willie knew that Tom was incognito and 'quite understood why they didn't write', Maria said Willie would 'no doubt be glad of a letter'. The fact that Tom had not written to Willie was most likely because he did not know how to extract himself from the situation in which he found himself. Maria's letter to Carrie was surprisingly intimate given that there is no evidence that they knew each other well.

About this time Tom became ill. It probably happened while he was at Briqueville-sur-Mer. He must have received the bad news about Willie from Carrie and this could have caused the illness. The situation was made worse when Charles Gogin wrote to Tom on 20th November. Alma Broadbridge must have told him of Tom's illness and Gogin's remark 'Try to get quite well for you know who's sake,' [134] must have filled Tom with horror at the thought that his relations with Maria Tuke were so widely rumoured. Tom had spoken to Gogin about Maria before he left London, [135] seeking his friend's reaction to a theoretical proposition rather than a reality. Tom was being propelled into a situation over which he had little control. He felt that he had prevaricated too long and determined to take a positive step and write to Dr. Tuke. One outcome of Willie's illness was that it had 'wonderfully reduced the parents' animosity against Tom'. [136] Tom made his request to Dr Tuke for permission to

133. Letter from Maria Tuke to Carrie Yates, 12th November 1880.

134. Letters from C. Gogin to T. C. Gotch, 20th November 1880.

135. Letter from C. Gogin to T. C. Gotch, 15th May 1881.

136. Letter from Maria Tuke to Jessie Gotch, 8th October 1880.

approach Maria shortly before Christmas and an exchange of letters followed. Tom must have written and told Willie of his action because in early January Willie wrote to say, 'Maria daren't send you a card this year', and 'my father goes back next week I think: he has not mentioned your letters, and I have hardly liked to introduce the subject'. [137] Fortunately Dr. Tuke was more sensible of events than the young people recognised and Tom's letters did not persuade him that the young man was really sure about his intentions; in the event he refused to give Tom permission to approach Maria formally.

Christmas 1880

Tom did not return to England for Christmas. He was in no mood for festivity and going home might have precipitated the business of Maria Tuke. Tom wrote to Harry Tuke to tell him that he intended to work throughout Christmas, although his brothers Henry and Alfred were to join him, no doubt bringing food parcels, diversions and family affection. Alma Broadbridge and Carrie Yates had gone home and Jane Ross was to join her brother 'to give her eyes a rest'. Harry was intent on working throughout Christmas too. 'I wonder if you feel as little like Xmas as I do?' he wrote 'It is very pleasant, we shall make up for lost time on the Sladites during their three weeks holiday'. But Harry was lonely and a little envious at the thought of Alfred turning up with hampers full of provisions:

> ' Is the grand grocer with you? Why does he not come on here and make some architectural studies, there is lots of material and I would have a knife and fork for his use and digging implements at his disposal. Why does not Miss Ross come here to recruit her eyes?' [138]

Tom was not in the mood for company. According to his mother, his brothers did not see much of him [139] as he spent most of the holiday in his studio working. Was he keeping away from them in case they challenged him about his intentions towards Maria Tuke? On Christmas eve they congregated in Tom's studio, forcing him to join their festivities. Charles Gogin was obviously intrigued,

137. Letter from W. S. Tuke to T. C. Gotch, 5th January 1881

138. Letter from H. S. Tuke to T. C. Gotch, 22nd December 1880.

139. Letter from Mary Ann Gotch to T. C. Gotch, 10th January 1881.

> 'It was very interesting to imagine your Christmas evening at
> the Studio. I hope you all enjoyed it. I am sure you must have
> done so if you were fairly well. Are you all right now?' [140]

How had Gogin heard? Most likely through Alma Broadbridge who
was in Carrie's confidence and Carrie would have had letters from
Tom while she was away. Nearly everyone knew that Tom and Carrie regularly wrote to each other and knew each other's whereabouts
although this does not seem to have raised any suspicion that their
friendship was other than platonic. For example, when Harry Tuke
wrote to Carrie after Christmas, saying, 'I should think you enjoyed
escaping from your banishment for a short time', he enclosed the
letter in a note to Tom, explaining 'I am sending this to Tom, as I
am not quite sure of your address'. [141]

Willie wrote to Tom after Christmas and was barely able to
hide his disappointment that Tom had not returned to England for
the holidays. Willie was still very ill and must have had a premonition that the husband he wanted for Maria was getting away.

> 'I hope the home contingent has made your Xmas pass pleas-
> antly: you would be quite a considerable party, and doubtless a
> merry one: I think Harry [Henry Gotch] shares your taste for
> the female sex, doesn't he? I don't blame him if he does, and
> you would have very favourable specimens of it if, as I sup-
> pose, the girls did not return home.' [142]

As the next three months progressed this premonition must have
grown as Tom failed to respond to either Willie's or Harry's suggestions that they should organise something for the next summer
vacation.

Facing up

Between Christmas and Easter Tom regained his common sense and
sorted out his romantic affairs. Perhaps Miss Thornely decided that
Tom was no longer 'a young knave', that 'the war' was won, that
'employment' was possible and that 'the King' lacked not
'subjects;' perhaps Miss Thornely had become less prickly? How

---

140. Letter from C. Gogin to T. C. Gotch, 28th December 1833

141. Letter from H. S. Tuke to C. B. Yates, 16th January 1881

142. Letter from W. S. Tuke to T. C. Gotch, 5th January 1881.

did this happen? If their romance had started in 1878, at the beginning of that first year at the Slade, it was a secret that they did not share with anyone; perhaps the relationship was construed by both as an expression of the 'free thought' that was discussed at the club? In later life both Tom and Caroline kept their personal affairs quite separate from work. They were recognised as very private people. Was this the reason for the secrecy? Jane Ross, who was very close to Tom, may have guessed the secret early on and after her initial disappointment that the role of wife was not hers, decided to befriend them both. She would have kept their secret close. Tom might have hinted at the relationship to Charles Gogin although the latter did not pick up the hint.

Tom was drawn into the Maria Tuke affair by both his idealism and his weakness. He had a strong sense of chivalry which could lead to determined but ill-conceived action. Once he had advertised his commitment to a course of action, he found it 'unmanly' to change his mind. He was also a kind man who did not like to disappoint other people who had high expectations of him. I believe that these aspects of his personality drew him into the 'near engagement' to Maria Tuke.

After Christmas, Tom continued to direct his energy to the picture he was painting for the Academy, but this must be the topic of another story. He was in London by 22nd March to attend a private view of the picture before it was sent to the Academy on the receiving day. Unfortunately it fared no better than the work of most of his friends and both Tom's picture 'The Prelude' and Tuke's picture 'The Bronzista Shop' were rejected. Tuke blamed the hanging committee, which he later said consisted 'of men rapidly going downhill, and two already arrived at the bottom.' [143]

In the meantime, Carrie was ill with a throat infection that she had picked up in London. She was no better in February and by the end of March, her condition had deteriorated. Perhaps the illness was linked to Tom's inability to bring the Maria Tuke affair to a conclusion. Tom's concern for Caroline was too intense to sit comfortably on a man who was publicly committed to marriage with someone else. Carrie's friends Alma and Jane must have known

---

143. Letter from Harry Tuke to Unknown, April 1883 (Sainsbury, 1933:66)

about the situation as the brunt of nursing her fell on them. Tom, who was on location at Briqueville-sur-Mer, was in constant communication with them about her condition. The following postcard from Jane Ross to Tom Gotch was dated 23rd February 1881.

'I send a post card as I see you are suffering anxiety for which there is not the slightest cause', wrote Jane Ross in late February. 'C wrote to you on the day I did, went out afterwards for a drive, went out again to dine at the Safiter, spent the next day in the country, and came back to the Montesquieu, when I met her. She proposes working this week. Yesterday again she had an engagement, which is as well, as both of them would be the better of change from the air of that hotel. Do not imagine that I would send you a false report, as an over sanguine one would be. I have still some conscience, though I have known Bohemians so long. On the contrary I would write to you if there were the slightest cause for anxiety. I have only time for a p.c. at present, having heaps to do' [144]

One suspicion must be that the three young women worked together to force Tom to sort out the situation once and for all. When he was in London in March he received a letter from Jane Ross that indicated that his relationship with Carrie was official—even if it was only Jane that knew. She wrote from the Hotel de Paris to say Caroline was ill and could not write herself. Was this true? Tom was in London where he was hosting the private view of his Academy paintings. The letter speaks for itself.

'Do you know I very much resent your departing without telling me your great news? Carrie was "beaucoup plus gentille" than you, and told me as soon as we came downstairs that evening. I would not therefore be writing to you now but that she has had a sharp attack of neuralgia and is unable to do so herself. She sends you a message that if she is able to be up she will write to you this afternoon, in the meantime I am feebly trying to supply her place, in case of your being too much surprised at not receiving letters, as I believe your habit is to write to one another three or four times a day. Yesterday I found her really suffering a great deal and in the evening though the pain was very much less, she was pulled down by it, and exceedingly weak. Miss Leslie brought her to see a doctor, which was

144. Postcard from Jane Ross to T. C. Gotch, 23rd February 1881.

sensible, for a Bohemian, then she came back with her and stayed with her till Alma's return. In the evening I came and Felix, who is far from well himself poor fellow. Alma sat with [her] till she fell asleep, which was not till four in the morning I am sorry to say. Now Alma has gone to hear Lefebre's criticism, and I am sitting by Carrie in her stead … She wants to know if you got the letters she sent you from your studio?

A letter from you has just arrived and she is completely absorbed. I believe I might do anything I liked in the room while the reading of that letter lasts, indeed I am seriously thinking of going over to the studio and coming back in an hour or two. I have just requested her to dictate messages and here they are. "I am so glad to get his letter". She is laughing now and can't say anything more. This is too bad, what culpable waste of time, oh here is another "I shall write to him today – some time". Now she says "That's all". So I think I shall say "That's all" too, and wish you good-bye. Do not be uneasy about her, I feel sure that the attack is over, and that she will be all right in a day or two, perhaps even today. She is well looked after, as a Bohemian is sure to be. [145]

If Jane had not intervened, would Tom have had the courage to go through with the break from Maria? Was Caroline behind Jane's letter? One day after he received this letter, Tom received the following from Willie who was still completely oblivious of the fact that Tom had decided not to marry Maria.

'I suppose you will be in London this morning and be thinking what a black murky place it looks after bright clean Paris. I hope the picture will look well in English air! If you get my Father to go to see it, wouldn't it be a good plan for Clark to be there at the same time – seeing that Father has a great idea of him? By the bye my Father has just had a box stolen containing, besides cash, valuable papers – valuable to him I mean, – and various private things. This will naturally have annoyed him considerably, so that perhaps the present moment might not be a propitious one for introducing a certain question, but you will see. [146]

Tom did not confess to Dr Tuke that he was withdrawing his suit to

145. Letter from Jane Ross to T. C. Gotch, circa 23rd March 1881.

146. Letter from W. S. Tuke to T. C. Gotch, 24th March 1881.

Maria so perhaps Dr Tuke did not attend Tom's private view. Immediately the RA had received his picture on 29th March, Tom left London for Kettering. Mary Ann Gotch's letter to Tom on 2nd May [147] suggests that he did not talk about his personal intentions to his mother and there is no evidence that he confided in his brothers. Although he saw one or two of his friends in London, like Charles Gogin, he did not confide in them either. In fact it is surprising that Gogin did not have prior wind of the affair as he was in frequent correspondence with Alma Broadbridge whom he later married. But perhaps Charles Gogin was keeping quiet?

Tom returned to Paris and visited Barbizon with Alma and Carrie. Tom wrote enthusiastically to Harry Tuke about the visit, but did not tell him about his change of matrimonial plans. That he was reluctant to write because he was fearful it would be the end of their friendship is suggested in a letter that Tom wrote to Caroline about this time. [148] Was he preparing the ground so that his friend would not be too surprised? Surely Harry was suspicious, with letters so full of Carrie Yates? In May, Harry's return letter suggested that he was suspicious but unwilling to ask outright what was going on.

> 'When you next write make sketch of your plans for the next nine months, the first three or four specially, it would be nice if we could go somewhere together in the summer for a bit, but where and when? It seems probable that the family may go to Newquay for the summer where I think of joining them in the beginning of July' [149]

Returning to Paris from Barbizon, Tom immediately left again for Briqueville-sur-Mer. Still he prevaricated. He could not make a general announcement about Caroline before Willie had the news; he could not confess to Willie and Harry until Dr. Tuke had been informed. He could not bring himself to write to Dr. Tuke. In the meantime Caroline was becoming anxious and her health was suffering; her friends Jane and Alma were critical of

---

147. Letter from Mary Ann Gotch to T. C. Gotch, 2nd May 1880.

148. Letter from T. C. Gotch to C. B. Yates, May 1881 (Rezelman, 1984:27 Footnote 53.)

149. Letter from H. S. Tuke to T. C. Gotch, 4th May 1881

Tom's procrastination. Tom turned to his friend Charles Gogin and came clean about the whole affair. Gogin wrote back immediately to give his blessing to Tom and also sent a letter to Alma explaining what had happened. Alma took the matter in hand and immediately sent a postcard to Tom on 23rd May. Reading between the lines of the short postcard that Alma Broadbridge sent Tom, there is no doubt about Caroline's frustration and anxiety and the relief felt by all three women at the news from Charles Gogin that Tom was at last sorting out the affair.

> 'I daresay you will be glad to hear from another person that Carrie is now quite herself again. I am glad all your tiresome business is getting so satisfactorily arranged and hope it won't be long before we see you back. I know you've heard from Gogin; in my letter he says "It did surprise me at first! But on reflection it is but natural etc. ... [150]

Epilogue

Alma's postcard may have been designed to reinforce Gogin's letter. If this is true it supports the theory that Carrie, Jane, Alma and Charles Gogin realised that Tom would not act without some forceful encouragement. Gogin's letter was persuasive enough. He said that he was not surprised at the turn in events because Tom had not acted as if he were in love with Maria and had been much too calm and took too intellectual a view of the matter.

> 'That you had unbounded respect for her character and for the capabilities of her mind was perfectly obvious, but of real love there wasn't (in the ordinary sense of the word) one little bit to be seen by an outsider. This time it is a very different affair! ... and I don't envy you the task before you of advising the last quotations of the market to your friends at Weston! That's the terrible art of the business! ... I shouldn't fret myself too much if I were you, about the effect your communication may have on M.T., as judging by the family temperament, it is very likely she quite shared your view of the subject and was not really in love with you any more than you were with her. At least let us hope so. I suppose the only one you care about besides her is W.T. and if he is the broadly minded and philosophical individual I take him to be you will stand pretty much with him as you

150. Postcard from WB to T. C. Gotch, 23rd May 1881.

have hitherto. As for mamma of course, elle jettera des hauts cris. But then that doesn't much matter as she would do that respecting any course you might take.' [151]

Tom wrote to Dr. Tuke as soon as he had had Gogin's letter. Dr. Tuke's reply indicated that he had recently written to Tom enquiring about Tom's intentions. Perhaps Dr. Tuke was also aware of Tom's temperament and had made a positive move to help him come clean. His letter to Tom was restrained, assuring Tom that he could make every allowance for Tom's withdrawal of the request made in his former letter.

'I could not rid myself of the impression of late that very possibly under your present circumstances a change of wish might have taken place, and hence my enquiry. Of course it would have been well if all we have passed through, could have been saved us, but for myself and I think I may speak for Mrs. Tuke, we shall always have a kindly feeling towards you and an interest in your welfare. Having changed your intention, you have asked in the most honourable manner and also in the most agreeable one. More I cannot say. With regard to Maria as we have not spoken to her, and as your letter distinctly left your relations as only those of friendship, I do not think you need express more to her than that you fear she may have got to think you intended more, and that if so you wrote for her to know from yourself that you have other thoughts and intentions. As I think that if she saw your handwriting addressed to her, she would be likely to think the contents of the letter different from what she would find them to be, it will be better for you to enclose it to Willy and ask him to tell her before handing it to her that you wish to explain what may otherwise be misunderstood. If she got it at breakfast with the other letters it would be very embarrassing.

Postscript: I have hardly perhaps expressed sufficiently my own regret that Maria should suffer any pain if such should be the case but I am not able to judge what impression she may have indirectly received as to your feelings.' [152]

Dr Tuke's postscript suggests that he was aware of Maria's possible pain. Maria was silent about the matter in her biography of her

151. Letter from C. Gogin to T. C. Gotch, 15th May 1881.

152. Letter from Daniel Hack Tuke to T. C. Gotch, 19th May 1881.

brother, but many years later she told her granddaughter that she was very upset and deeply regretted losing Tom. [153] Harry Tuke did not learn about the matter until later. He had moved from Florence to Pietra Santa, and so did not get Tom's letter immediately. Willie did not write to Tom until a month later, claiming an indisposition. His letter was close to Gogin's prediction, saying that one could not judge for other people in these matters and that love like the wind 'bloweth whither it listeth'.

> 'I could wish you had shown a little more stability', wrote Willie, 'it annoys me to picture the horrid grin of triumph, which will suffuse the meek features of W. H. Hills Esq., and the similar satisfaction, which will be shown by the Rheam tribe when they learn what has happened.' [154]

In July 1881 Tom Gotch and Caroline Yates returned to London. Caroline met Tom's family in Kettering. They were married on 31st August 1881, in Newlyn. Harry Tuke was back in England but did not attend the wedding. The Tuke family were in Clifton, 'a vile ugly town' with hideous people, wrote Harry.[155] Maria wrote saying 'My blessings to you, I wish I were going to Newlyn'. [156]

Tom and Carrie were married at St Peter's Church Newlyn and the wedding was witnessed by Carrie's sister Ess and Tom's brother Alfred as well as Frank Bodilly who was to marry Ess, and Annie Tonkin from Newlyn. It was a happy affair that was popular with the local fishing community who made a 'spontaneous demonstration of affection' that provoked Edward Yates, Carrie's father, to remark that 'people seldom receive such notice of love who do not love'. [157]

The Long Engagement had ended at last.

---

153. Price, 2001:6

154. Letter from W. S. Tuke to T. C. Gotch, 17th June 1881.

155. Letter from H. S. Tuke to T. C. Gotch, 20th July 1881. (Sainsbury, 1933:52)

156. Letter from Maria Tuke to Carrie Yates, 16th August 1881

157. Letter from Edward Yates to T. C. Gotch (Rezelman, 1884: 119)

CERTIFIED COPY of an
ENTRY OF MARRIAGE

Pursuant to the
Marriage Act 1949

Registration District _Penzance_

1381, Marriage solemnized at _St. Peter's Church_
Parish
District of _St Peter's Newlyn_ in the _County of Cornwall_

No.	When married	Name and surname	Age	Condition	Rank or profession	Residence at the time of marriage	Father's name and surname
	1	2	3	4	5	6	7
65	Aug 31	Thomas Cooper Gotch	26	Bachelor	Artist	Newlyn	Thomas Henry Gotch
		Caroline Burland Yates	25	Spinster	—	Newlyn	Edward Yates

Married in the _Parish Church_ according to the _Rites and Ceremonies of the Established Church_ by _hic_

This marriage was solemnized between us, { Thomas Cooper Gotch / Caroline Burland Yates } in the presence of us, { E.B. Yates A. Tonkin Frank Boddy / T. Alfred Gotch }

H. Skrine Assistant

Certified to be a true copy of an entry in a register in my custody, _Rita A. Collier_ Registrar

Superintendent Registrar

Date _28th August 2001_

ACKNOWLEDGEMENTS & THANKS

Thanks to the Tate Britain, London for giving access to their archive of letters and papers relating to Thomas Cooper Gotch and his contemporaries and for their permission to reproduce a facsimile of part of a letter of H. S. Tuke.

Thanks to the Alfred East Gallery, Kettering for giving access to their archive of papers and exhibition catalogues and for their permission to reproduce the picture, Abraham and Isaac with the Angel. The Alfred East Gallery houses a collection of 35 paintings by Thomas Cooper Gotch which are available for viewing by appointment. Telephone 01536 534219; Fax 01536 534370.

Thanks to the private collectors who wish to remain anonymous who provided information and gave their permission for material, photographs and pictures to be used in this booklet. Particular thanks for the generous permission to reproduce the painting on the cover of the booklet.

Thanks to Alan Shears, Shears Fine Art Gallery, 58 Chapel Street, Penzance for access to his archive and permission to use the story, 'A Long Engagement'. Shears Fine Art Gallery specialises in paintings by T. C. Gotch and other artists of the Newlyn School.

Thanks to Christopher Gotch, for access to his family archive and permission to reproduce illustrations from his book and for his enthusiasm and support.

Thanks to Robin Hanbury-Tenison for access to his archive and permission to reproduce 'Monseigneur Love'.

Thanks to Charles Clarke for permission to reproduce the drawing of Jessie Gotch.

Thanks to Brian Price who compiled and edited Artists Letters, a collection of letters to and from artists most of whom were contemporary with Gotch, which has been deposited in the National Archive at the Tate Britain and for his advice on aspects of the booklet.

Thanks to Paul Gotch who is a marvellous proof-reader.

Finally thanks to Ron Hogg for his long hours of research without which the compilation of the booklet would have been impossible.

BIBLIOGRAPHY

Gotch, Christopher (2000), *Thomas Cooper Gotch: the artist's life and work*, Privately Published by the Author.

Hepburn, Bruce (1994) *Thomas Cooper Gotch: the making of the artist*, Published Alfred East Gallery, Kettering.

Jacomb-Hood, George Percy (1925) *With Brush and Pencil*, London, Albermarle St: John Murray

Forbes-Robertson, Sir Johnston (1925). *A Player Under Three Reigns*, London

Price, Brian D. (2001) *The Club*, Unpublished Paper.

Rezelman, Betsy Cogger (1984) *The Newlyn Artists and their Place in Late Victorian Art*, University Microfilms International.

Sainsbury, Maria Tuke (1933) *Henry Scott Tuke: a memoir*, London, Martin Secker.

Spanton, W. S. (1864) *An Art Student and His Teachers in the Sixties*, F. B. Cartoon, Reprinted Landon: Robert Scott 1927.

Sparrow, Walter Shaw (1925) *Memories of Life and Art through Sixty Years*, John Lane The Bodley Head Ltd

LIST OF WORKS BY T. C. GOTCH 1877-1881

Boat by the Side of a Lake. Etching, 9.5 x 15 cm, circa 1877. Hanbury-Tenison Collection.

Four Heads. Etching, 7 x 10.5 cm, signed, circa 1877. State Gallery of Victoria Permanent Collection.

Girl with a Stick. Etching, 5 x 4.6 cm, circa 1877. Hanbury-Tenison Collection.

Self Portrait. Pencil, 57 cm diameter, circa 1877. Alfred East Gallery, Kettering Permanent Collection.

La Dilicienie Turelli, Bruges. Watercolour, circa 1878. Exhibited Royal Scottish Academy 1880 (889).

Courtyard of the Maison Plantin. Watercolour, 47 x 41 cm, circa 1878. Alfred East Gallery, Kettering Permanent Collection.

Streatley Mill, Bedfordshire. Watercolour, 36 x 47 cm, dated 1878.

(Referenced, Kettering Archive).

La Belle Dame sans Merci. Etching, 18 x 23 cm, signed, dated 1879. State Gallery of Victoria Permanent Collection.

Nude Woman Kneeling on the Seashore. Etching, 20 x 15 cm, signed, circa 1879. Hanbury-Tenison Collection.

Abraham and Isaac with angel. Grisaille, 44 x 31 cm, signed, circa 1879. Alfred East Gallery, Kettering Permanent Collection.

Head of Boy. Etching, 20 x 15 cm, circa 1879. Private Collection.

Figure Study. Pencil, circa 1879. (Referenced, Rezelman, 1984).

Head of Youth. Etching, circa 1879. (Referenced, Kettering Archive).

Sidmouth. Watercolour, circa 1879. Exhibited RA 1880 (903).

Landscape after a Legros. Etching, circa 1879. (Referenced, Rezelman, 1984).

By the Coast, Cornwall. Watercolour, signed, dated 1879. Exhibited, The Rustic Image: rural themes in British Painting, 1880-1912, November 1979.

Head of Bearded Man. Brown pencil, 19.5 x 15 cm, circa 1879. Private Collection.

Le Repas des Pauvres. Etching, circa 1879. (Referenced, Kettering Archive).

Full Length Nude Man with Moustache. Pencil, 56 x 32 cm, circa 1879-1880. Hanbury-Tenison Collection.

Nude Woman Seated. Pencil, 28 x 33 cm, circa 1879-1880. Hanbury-Tenison Collection.

Study of Clasped Hands on Lap. Charcoal, 16.5 x 25 cm, circa 1879-1880. Hanbury-Tenison Collection.

Monseigneur Love. Oil on canvas, 79 x 99 cm, signed, dated 1880. Hanbury-Tenison Collection.

Head of Bearded Man with Headband. Etching, 15 x 20 cm, signed, dated 1880. State Gallery of Victoria Permanent Collection.

Pine Trees with Artist Painting. Etching, 13 x 9 cm, signed, circa 1880. State Gallery of Victoria Permanent Collection.

Miss Yates as a Fishergirl. Oil, 20 x 11.5 cm, signed, circa 1880. Exhibited, Artists of the Newlyn School 1880-1900, Newlyn Orion Gallery, 1958 (50).

Nurse and Child. Oil, 91 x 74 cm, signed, circa 1880. Exhibited, Artists of the Newlyn School 1880-1900, Newlyn Orion Gallery, 1958 (51).

Study of a Head. Signed, circa 1880. Exhibited RA 1880 (1293).

Portrait of Jessie Robinson. Oil on canvas, circa 1880. Charles Clarke Collection.

Miss Caroline Burland Yates. Oil, 20 x 11.5 cm, signed, circa 1880. Exhibited, Artists of the Newlyn School 1880-1900, Newlyn Orion Gallery, 1958 (49).

A Stranded Collier. Exhibited Royal Scottish Academy 1880 (653).

Under a Spell. Exhibited Liverpool Autumn Exhibition 1881 (390).

An Interior. Exhibited, Salon, Paris 1881.

Jessie Robinson. Pencil, 19 x 14 cm, dated 1881. Charles Clarke Collection.

The Prelude. Oil on canvas, 101 x 81 cm, signed, dated 1881. Private Collection.

Caroline Gotch sketching near Brolles, Oil on board, 20 x 13 cm, circa 1881. (Auction, 18.7.2001).

Portrait of Millard. Circa 1881/2. (Referenced, Rezelman, 1984).

Portrait of Wainwright. Circa 1881/2. (Referenced, Rezelman, 1984).

Drying Sails: Saturday Morning. Oil. Exhibited Royal Society of British Artists 1881/2 (410)

I Told You So. Oil, Exhibited, Royal Society of British Artists 1881/2 (395)

Panel. Exhibited, Royal Society of British Artists 1881/2 (558).

INDEX OF NAMES

Berrill, Frank. 30.
Bodilly, Frank. 70.
Broadbridge, Alma. 3,31-32,34-35, 37,49,61-64,66-68.
Burne-Jones. 26.
Butler, Samuel. 40, 44, 46-50.
Clark, Joseph Benwell. 19,21,24, 26,36,40-43,66.
Conway, Dr Moncure Daniel. 16-17.
Crosfield, Jessie. 32-33.
Doherty, Pat. 1.
Dowdeswell, Messrs. 26.
Durham, Mr. 2.
Dyer, Samuel. 30.

Farr, Henrietta. 3,30,32,43,48,49.
Festing-Jones, Henry. 48,50.
Ford, Emma. 31-32,34-35.
Fox, R. 57.
Gale, Uncle Sam. 14-15.
Gogin, Charles. 32,37,47,59,61-62, 64, 67-70.
Gotch, Caroline see Yates, Caroline Burland
Gotch, Davis. 43.
Gotch, Dr. Fredrick. 20.
Gotch, Francis. 20,30,32,34.
Gotch, Henry Gale. 14,16-17,41,55, 62-63.

Gotch, Jessie. 51-55,57.
Gotch, John Alfred. 3,14,17,20,24, 51,53,57,62,70.
Gotch, Katie. 20.
Gotch, Mary Ann. 26,60,67.
Gotch, Maud. 43.
Gotch, Phyllis 1,55.
Gotch, Rose Muriel. 43.
Goulding, F. 19,26-27.
Haweis. 16
Hepburn, Fanny. 14-15.
Hepburn, Josephine. 20-21,24.
Hepburn, Mary Ann (Gotch) 'Aunt Thomas'. 20.
Hepburn, Thomas 'Uncle Thomas'. 20.
Hepburn, Tom. 20,24.
Hewitt, Miss. 30.
Hills, Mr and Mrs. 56,70.
Horsley, Rosamund (Gotch). 32.
Horsley, Victor. 30-32,34-36,40,44.
Jacomb-Hood, George Percy. 16, 19, 21-22,59.
Keo, Miss. 30.
Laurens, Jean Paul. 58-61.
Laurie, D. Edward. 30.
Laurie, Gertrude. 26,56.
Lawrence, Samuel. 1-2.
Legros, Professor Alphonse. 2,19, 26,27.
Martin, Henry. 23.
Mill, J. S. 55
Morley, Robert. 31.
Naughten, Miss. 30,37.
Paget, Henry. 3,30-32,36,43,46-50.
Paget, Sidney. 3,30.
Paget, Walter. 3,30.
Parkyn. 37
Paul of Kegan Paul. Mr. 46.
Poynter. 26.
Radford, Ernest. 34.
Rathbone, Harold. 3,18,30,45,47-48.
Rheam family. 53,70.
Robinson, Edward. 20.
Robinson, Katy see Gotch
Robinson, Maria. 20,56.
Robinson, Josephine see Hepburn

Rosenberg, Miss. 35.
Ross, Jane. 3,14,16-18,21,30-31, 33-35,37,44-45,49,62,64-68.
Sainsbury, Gertrude. 34.
Sainsbury, Harrington. 31-32,34.
Santley, Bo. 34,40-42,49,57.
Santley, Charles. 40,49-51,57.
Santley, Edith. 34-35,40-42,49-52,57.
Santley, Mic. 40.
Sargeant, Mary. 34-35.
Savage, Elizabeth. 46.
Skeete, De Courcey. 34,37.
Slinger, Mr. 19
Smith, J. H. 44.
Sparrow, Walter. 3.
Strang, William. 20.
Tayler, A. Chevallier. 3,30,59.
Thompson, William. 34-36.
Tonkin, Annie. 70.
Tregelles, Lydia. 22.
Tuke, Dr Daniel Hack. 20,22,52,57, 61,66-67,69.
Tuke, Henry Scott. 19,21-24,26,31, 34,36, 40-43,45,48-53,56,59,62-64, 67,70.
Tuke, Maria. 20-22,32,34,49-64,66-70.
Tuke, Mrs. 55-56,69.
Tuke, William Samuel. 16,20,22, 30-36,38,44,49,51-63,66-67,69, 70.
Uren, J. C. 23.
Urquart, Mrs. 34,36.
Verlat, Professor Charles. 2
Waterhouse. 26.
Wedmore, Ernest. 34.
Wedmore, Isabel. 35.
Wedmore, Mary. 54.
Whistler, James McNeill. 16,26.
Whymper, C. 26
Wilks, Mark. 16.
Wills, Arthur. 21.
Yates, Caroline Burland. 1-4,13-14, 21,23,30-32,34,37-38,40-45,48-50,52,55,57,59-70.
Yates, Edward. 3-4,70.
Yates, Ess. 3,23,34,40,48,70.
Yates, Margaret. 3.